CORE BUSINESS STUDIES

ECONOMICS

R. Maile BA, CERT.ED.

Mitchell Beazley

The producers of Core Business Studies
wish to thank those members of the
British Institute of Management who have
given their advice and their time to ensure
that each book in the series meets the high
standards required by modern British
business.

Published 1983 by Mitchell Beazley Publishers
87-89 Shaftesbury Avenue, London W1V 7AD

© Mike Morris Productions Limited 1983

Produced for Mitchell Beazley by
Mike Morris Productions Ltd.
Burnham House, 93a High Street, Burnham, Bucks.

ISBN 0 85533 444 4

Designed by Stewart Cowley & Associates
Typeset by Barnes Design + Print Group
Printed and bound in Great Britain.

Contents

Introduction

Economics presents an interesting paradox. On the one hand, the media and political attention have highlighted the importance of economic developments such as inflation, unemployment, taxation and interest rates. This is quite natural since such factors impinge on all our living standards. On the other hand, public awareness of the causes and significance of economic change seems no better informed now than it has ever been. Indeed, there even seems to be some strange and frightful mystery about the subject, which acts as a barrier to people's understanding or even to their will to understand.

Two main factors seem to contribute to this unfortunate and undesirable situation. Firstly, traditional means of introducing the subject have been strongly biased to theoretical models, the relevance of which to the real world has not been sufficiently explained. Secondly, access to the subject has been hampered by an obscure terminology and the use of complex diagrammatical representation.

It cannot be claimed that this book completely overcomes such difficulties, but a considerable effort has been made to reduce these barriers. Since business studies is determinedly practical in its approach, it has been possible to reduce the time spent in developing theories, and to concentrate more on the significance of their conclusions. Where appropriate, some elements of traditional ,theory have either been completely omitted or treated in a critical manner, as a basis for elaborating alternative means of understanding a particular subject.

Terminology and diagrammatical representation are more demanding problems, since they form the basis of concise and effective communication. Terms are, however, carefully explained and a detailed glossary is provided as a ready source of reference. Diagrams have been kept as simple and informative as possible, and the use of a second colour in their printing is intended to further clarify the diagrams and to ease understanding.

This book has been written as one of a series, each considering different aspects of the business world and the decision-making process. Much of this particular book is concerned with what might be called the firm's 'environment': setting the scene within which companies operate, and explaining the reasons for changes in that environment and their effects on the business sector.

The book is intended for those who are studying economics formally for the first time, whether as part of an A-level or introductory degree course in Business Studies, or as part of a BEC course or professional examination.

Any economics text requires careful reading, especially where ideas have been expressed as concisely as the format of this series dictated. One of the features of this series is the use of **bold type** to focus attention on the main points, and it is hoped that this will also be helpful when the book is used as a revision aid. Indeed, it is often helpful, before commencing a detailed study of a chapter, to flick through its pages noting the main headings to get a better idea of the structure of the argument.

The economic environment is a dynamic one. The pace of change is such that no text can hope to be timeless. Students are therefore well advised to keep themselves informed of current developments by regular reading of a 'quality' newspaper and by watching the two or three first-rate current affairs programmes on television or listening to informed commentary on the radio. In many senses, the purpose of an introductory text such as this is to foster a critical understanding of economic principles so as to provide the means whereby students can understand and evaluate such contemporary developments. I hope this book will go some way towards meeting this objective.

Acknowledgements
I would like to thank Dick Knowles and Eddie Martin, the series editors, for their helpful and constructive suggestions which assisted the preparation of the final manuscript. My thanks also to the Controller of Her Majesty's Stationery Office for permission to reproduce abstracts from official statistics.

Finally, I should acknowledge a continuing debt to the wit and wisdom of my students, past and present, who have collectively corrected the errors of judgement I would otherwise have made. For such errors that do remain, I must of course accept full responsibility.

Chapter 1

The Economic Perspective

Economics is the study of certain aspects of the consequences of scarcity. It is apparent that man's material desires far exceed his capacity to produce goods and services, and that it is therefore necessary to make choices. Thus, decision-making is at the heart of economic studies. Economists are concerned with the implications of decisions about how society's scarce resources are used to satisfy particular wants.

Choice and opportunity cost

In order to make choices, there is a need to determine priorities. Once a choice has been made, there is an inevitable sacrifice expressed in terms of what has been forgone. For example, a firm may have some spare factory space which it could use either to extend its production line or to improve its despatch facilities. Indeed, there may be many other options too. When the firm has determined its priorities and decided on one use for the spare space, the *best* alternative use forgone is described as the **opportunity cost** of using the space as decided.

Opportunity cost is the *real cost* of having something, measured in physical rather than money terms. It results directly from the fact of scarcity: sacrifice is only necessary if you cannot have everything you want. Man appears to have an insatiable capacity to extend his wants: as soon as some are satisfied, new aspirations are formed, and so the decision-making process continues.

Scarce resources

In economics, anything which has an opportunity cost is described as scarce. There are few resources or goods which do not have an opportunity cost. One example might be air (but not *fresh* air), which is therefore described as a **free good.** This is not to be confused with goods and services for which no price is charged directly to the consumer, such as public libraries and parks. These obviously do have an opportunity cost, and so are termed **zero-priced goods.**

The resources available to man for the purpose of satisfying wants are conventionally classified into four groups:

1. Land In economics this has a wider meaning than in everyday usage. It is best described as 'nature's bounty', i.e. all non-human resources which occur naturally, from mineral deposits, forests and soil to gases in the air. In many cases these resources are not available freely: other resources may be needed to extract them for man's use (e.g. mining).

2. Labour This can be defined as 'the mental and physical effort of humans in the course of production'.

3. Capital This also has a precise economic meaning, which should not be confused with the everyday use of the word. It may be defined as 'goods which are not used for current consumption', and may be sub-divided into:

  (a) Producer durable-use goods, i.e. goods which yield services over a period of time and are used to make other goods, e.g. factories and machines.
  (b) Producer single-use goods, i.e. goods used to make other goods and services which are used up in the course of production (or are transformed so that they may not be repeatedly used for the same purpose), e.g. bricks and mortar.
  (c) Stocks These comprise holdings of raw materials, unsold consumer goods and part-finished goods (or 'work in progress').

4. Enterprise Defined as 'the factor which bears the risks of production', enterprise is the least readily quantified of the factors of production and has the distinguishing characteristic that it is the only factor which may earn a negative return (i.e. a loss). Whilst many **entrepreneurs** perform other functions, such as management, it is the risk-bearing element which is the defining characteristic. For example, a shareholder in I.C.I. may take no part at all in the day-to-day running of the company but, in bearing part of the risks of production, is clearly an entrepreneur. If the company spends more in hiring factor services than it receives from selling its output, the company will make a loss and the shareholder will receive no dividend: in the event of the company's liquidation, he stands to lose his initial subscription to the company's capital.

Factor mobility
The economy's scarce resources have alternative uses. As has been seen, resources put to one particular use have an opportunity cost – their forgone use elsewhere. However, in a dynamic economy, the priorities of individuals, firms and the society as a whole are subject to change. Factor mobility is the term used to describe the readiness with which factors may be redirected to alternative uses. The two main forms of factor mobility which are referred to are:

1. Occupational mobility The ease with which a factor may be transferred from one productive capacity to another in a diffferent industry.
2. Geographical mobility The ease with which factors' geographical locations may be changed.

Whilst these terms are most readily applied to labour, it should be apparent that they are equally applicable to the other factors (when correctly defined).

Production
Production involves bringing together the different factor services needed to make available the different goods and services which satisfy people's wants. It is commonly divided into three stages:

1. Primary production Industries involved in extracting raw materials.
2. Secondary production Manufacturing industry.

3. Tertiary production The distribution of manufactured goods and the supply of services.

Consumption

In economic terms, 'consumption' is best defined as 'using up' goods and services. From a consumer's viewpoint, a distinction can be made between:

1. Consumer durables Goods used by households which give repeated service over a period of time, e.g. cars and washing machines.
2. Consumer single-use goods Those which, as the name suggests, are used only once and cannot be re-used, such as petrol and washing powder.

Consumption can also be applied to the use of producer durable-goods. **Capital consumption** (or 'depreciation') is the process of using up part of the productive life of a producer durable.

ECONOMIC ORGANIZATION

All economies face the same basic economic problem of scarcity. Consequently, all economies have three basic decisions to make:

1. What goods to produce?
2. How should the goods be produced?
3. Who should receive the goods?

Although the problem is the same for all economies, the methods of organizing a country's economy vary widely and have come to be reflected in fundamental political differences.

Modern economies are based on the principle of the **division of labour** between different productive tasks. Rather than each family group operating a subsistence system in which it directly produces to meet its own needs, individuals specialize in a particular activity, trading their surplus produce for the surplus of other individuals. This principle of specialization and exchange has extended to sub-dividing tasks within the production of individual goods, and the use of money has facilitated the more efficient trading of individuals' specialized products. In consequence of this extension of the division of labour, the vast majority of workers in an economy are employed by firms or the State rather than working directly on their own behalf.

Although there are sophisticated refinements, the basic economic decisions outlined above are essentially made by two different methods: planning or the market mechanism. In most developed Western economies, the primary means of resource allocation is through the determination of prices, formed by the interaction of buyers and sellers in markets. A **market** exists wherever buyers and sellers of a good or service can interact: there is no necessity for them actually to meet one another. Thus, some markets consist of newspaper, radio or television advertisements placed by sellers, followed by postal or telephone transactions; others are conducted mainly by telex or telephone messages, and many still involve personal face-to-face contacts, ranging from the local street market to the Stock Exchange.

Exchange The principle of exchange is simple: each party seeks to further its own interests, so that an exchange will be agreed when it is considered to be to the *mutual* benefit of the parties involved. In a product market, for example, the consumer is aiming to satisfy a particular want, and will therefore take into account such factors as price (relative to that offered by other sellers), convenience, anticipated satisfaction, alternative goods which might be purchased and so on. The producer is aiming to make a profit and might consider factors such as the price buyers are prepared to pay relative to the cost of production, the possibility of greater profits by selling in different markets, the prices charged by producers of similar goods, etc. In the absence of *force majeure*, a transaction would signify the fulfilment of both parties' objectives.

Precisely the same principle applies in factor markets. A worker will consider the relative advantages of working for one company, or of being unemployed or self-employed, just as the employer will consider the relative benefits of employing one worker or another, or of substituting other factors in place of labour and so forth.

Decision-making via the market mechanism
In Figure 1, a hypothetical economic system is shown in which all the decisions – what, how and for whom to produce – result from the free interaction of buyers and sellers in markets. It is assumed that there is no direct government intervention in the economy. The model is divided into two sectors: the households, who own the economy's productive resources, and the business sector, which produces goods and services.

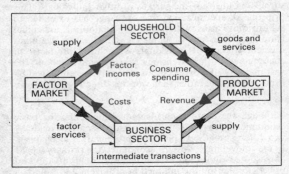

Figure 1. The price system

Two main flows are shown: a physical flow of goods and services, and a money flow representing payments for the goods and services. In order to produce, the business sector needs to buy factor services, and in order to consume, the households need to gain incomes by selling the factor services they own. Thus, there are two types of market:

1. Factor markets Where the households supply factor services, which are demanded by the business sector, in return for factor incomes.

2. Product markets Where the business sector supplies goods and services, which are demanded by the households, in return for payments which are termed 'consumption expenditure'. The diagram shows a third flow of intermediate transactions, where business units buy goods and services from each other as one stage in the production of goods and services for the household sector.

It is useful to make an initial assumption that every market is highly competitive: households seek to maximize their satisfaction and firms to maximize their profits; no individual consumer or firm is able to influence the market price; there is no collusion between households or business units. In each market a price would be formed by the free interaction of demand and supply. The equilibrium price for any good or service is the price at which the quantity consumers are able and willing to buy in a given time period is exactly matched by the quantity which producers are able and willing to supply. Should an individual firm try to charge a higher price, consumers will go to other firms selling the same product, and no firm will sell at a lower price since they can sell the quantity they wish at the prevailing market price (by definition). It is the existence of a large number of competing buyers and sellers in every market which prevents individual actions from affecting the market price.

This competitive market system is referred to by a variety of titles, the most usual being 'the price system'. Alternatives include the 'free market' economy or the 'private enterprise' system. The most significant feature of the model is that the basic economic decisions are made automatically as a result of the economic factors – consumers and firms – pursuing what they perceive to be their own best interests.

What to produce?

If consumers' demand for a good exceeds the quantity supplied at a given price, competition for the good between consumers will raise the price until an equilibrium is achieved. This is likely to result in higher than normal profits for the firms supplying the good, which will act as a signal for new firms to come into the market. This will require new factor services to be attracted into the market: an increase in demand, which will raise the price of the factor services involved, diverts some scarce resources from their alternative uses. As more firms compete to sell the increased output of the good, the price will tend to fall. This in turn reduces profits, and once these have reached what is considered a 'normal' level, there will no longer be an incentive for more firms to enter the industry. Similarly, the increased supply of factor services will be stemmed once the rewards to be earned have returned to a level which is insufficient to divert them from alternative uses.

The initial 'disequilibrium' in this example has triggered a series of reactions: the wishes of the consumers for more of the good have been satisfied, profits have reverted to a 'normal' level and more resources have been directed to the production of the good. All this has occurred without any co-ordinated planning or direction. The decision as to 'what to produce?' is made according to the demand of consumers: a situation sometimes referred to as **consumer sovereignty**.

How to produce?
It has been shown that the price for any good is determined in the market and cannot be influenced by the actions of an individual firm. Obviously, if each unit the firm sells costs it more to produce than the market price, the firm will make a loss and eventually go out of business. Thus, there is an incentive for firms to produce as efficiently as possible and thereby reduce their average costs. This will involve determining the best combination of factors and ensuring the best possible output from the chosen set of inputs. In this way, and again without co-ordinated planning or direction, the most efficient use of the economy's scarce resources is ensured.

For whom to produce?
Given that consumer demand determines what is produced, the key factor in deciding who gets what is the ability to pay. This is dependent on the incomes of consumers, which in turn are determined by the prices of the factor services which they are able to sell.

Advantages of the price system
The price system is an attractive theoretical proposition. Whilst the motive force is self-interest (i.e. profits for firms and satisfaction of wants for consumers), the result appears to be in the best interest of the society as a whole. Without coercion, resources are directed to where they are needed (and re-directed as demand changes over time), consumers get the goods they demand, competition prevents abnormal profits in the long run and resources are used to maximum efficiency.

However, it is readily apparent that the assumptions on which the model is based are unlikely to be exactly matched in any actual market. For example, some firms account for such a large share of individual markets that they can influence the market price by their own actions. In other markets, some firms or consumers might be inclined to act together ('collude') for this purpose. Thus most proponents of the market mechanism recognize the need for some element of government intervention in the economy to ensure that markets behave as if they were as competitive as the model suggests, and to protect consumer interests.

Given this proviso, the price mechanism remains the prime means of resource allocation in most western economies, and thousands of goods and services are produced and distributed in essentially the way the model predicts.

REASONS FOR GOVERNMENT INTERVENTION

However, governments intervene in economies for many reasons other than the maintenance of competitive forces. The size of the government's sphere of economic activity – known as the **public sector** – is often used as a political index of the country's character. For example, the Soviet Union's mix of planning and free market resource allocation tends far more towards centralized decision-making than does that of the U.S.A. Below, we summarize the main reasons why governments in essentially private enterprise economies have taken responsibility for certain aspects of economic activity.

1. Merit goods
In the price system, income determines the ability to buy goods and services. This may mean that some individuals cannot afford to buy goods and services which it is believed that everyone should have the opportunity to benefit from, regardless of their income. These 'merit goods' might include such items as health services, education, libraries, art galleries, etc.

The state can guarantee access to such goods and services in a variety of ways:

(a) **Direct provision** The state acts as entrepreneur and charges prices aimed at securing equality of opportunity. This may involve charging different prices according to individuals' income levels or providing the service at a zero or subsidized price (and financing its operation from general taxation, based on the ability of people to pay).
(b) **Indirect provision** Private firms produce the goods and services, but the state provides income supplements or vouchers for those who would not otherwise be able to afford the goods.

2. Welfare payments
The operation of the price mechanism may be modified by income supplements provided by the state for those who are least able to help themselves and whose standard of living might otherwise fall below a level the society considers acceptable. Examples of such welfare payments include unemployment benefits and state pensions.

3. Natural monopolies
A natural monopoly exists where an industry will operate most efficiently if there is only one producer in a given region: the usual examples are public utilities, such as water, gas and electricity supply. As in the case of merit goods, governments may intervene directly (by nationalizing production) or indirectly (by licencing private monopolies). In some countries the argument is extended to a wide range of

industries, such as airlines, steel production, motor vehicle production and extractive industries, e.g. coal and petroleum.

4. Social capital

Certain goods and services would either be difficult to price at all or pricing would actually decrease the benefit which could be derived from them. Road networks, for example, would be much less efficient if privately owned and subject to tolls at every turn. The problem of pricing access to national parks or of charging for the provision of street lamps is sufficiently great to warrant zero-priced provision for consumers, financed from different forms of taxation.

The term 'social capital' includes all the goods which are not used for current consumption and which are owned collectively by a nation. In addition to the items considered above, this might also include state universities and schools, state hospitals and so forth.

Many items of social capital could be termed 'collective or public goods', i.e. goods from which it is difficult to exclude others (apart from those willing to pay for the good) from enjoying the benefits. For example, if national defence was provided on a private enterprise basis, people who were not prepared to pay the asking price would still benefit from the protection provided for those who did pay. In such cases, there is an obvious advantage in centralized provision.

5. Externalities

The price system is amoral: it makes no value judgements on the relative merits of different goods. If the consumer is prepared to pay the price, the good or service will be provided. The government may wish to intervene in this process for one of two reasons:

(a) To protect people from themselves

On society's behalf, the government may intervene to control or prohibit goods which are considered to have a detrimental effect on the consumers, e.g. drugs or pornography.

(b) To protect people from the side-effects of others' actions

Decisions in the price system are made on the basis of self-interest: the producer weighs the costs he will incur against the revenue he stands to gain, and the consumer considers his anticipated satisfaction against the price he must pay and the opportunities forgone.

However, some production and consumption decisions will have side-effects on other people not directly involved in the decision (termed 'externalities' or 'social costs and benefits'). In the absence of government intervention, for example, a producer might be prepared to pollute nearby rivers or allow noxious fumes into the atmosphere if this reduces his costs. Similarly, a consumer might prefer to buy a lawnmower which disturbs the neighbourhood's television reception if this model was cheaper than one incorporating a suppressor. On the other hand, in a congested city a consumer may choose to use public transport rather than drive a private car, and this action tends to benefit other road users by helping to reduce congestion on the roads.

Where social costs exist there is, in the absence of government intervention, a tendency to greater production and consumption than would be considered desirable from society's viewpoint. Conversely, the effect of failing to take account of social benefits in production and consumption decisions is a lower level of welfare than would be possible if the externalities were reflected in the price of consumption.

Governments can intervene to encourage people to take account of these externalities in a number of ways:

(a) **Legal compulsion** This may take the form, for example, of placing limits on the permitted levels of atmospheric pollution.

(b) **Legal compensation** People may have the right to be compensated for detriment to their welfare caused by others' actions.

(c) **Internalization** The government may use taxes and subsidies to allow for the value of externalities in the prices charged to consumers.

(d) **Inverted justice** People whose welfare would suffer as the result of another's action might be prepared to pay the 'offender' not to inflict the social costs on them. This is a reversal of the usual legal principle that the offender should compensate the offended. An example might be where the residents in a neighbourhood pay the organizers of an open air pop festival not to hold a concert in their locality.

6. Aid for industry
Just as the government may look after individuals who are least able to help themselves, it may offer similar aid to firms. This may, for example, be aimed at ensuring a balanced regional development of industry within a country, to support industries in temporary financial difficulties or to protect firms from 'unfair' foreign competition.

7. Economic management
Many economists believe that the free market system, left to its own devices, would fail to secure the full employment of a nation's scarce resources. Thus, they consider that government intervention to control the level of economic activity over time is desirable. This 'demand management' may also be directed to controlling the balance of payments and the price-level, among other things. This may extend to more detailed forward planning of the economy to influence various aspects of resource allocation.

This list of reasons for government intervention is far from exhaustive and many aspects will be considered in more detail in subsequent chapters. There are, however, some important criticisms of the effects of government intervention which need to be mentioned:

(a) **Market discipline** Enterprise supported by or directly controlled by the state may tend to be less responsive to the incentives of profit and loss, since the state under- writes any losses incurred. Thus, if profit-making is as important a spur to competition and increased efficiency as the price system suggests, there is a danger that govern- ment intervention in production will lead to less than optimum efficiency. Moreover, since government- sponsored production often has monopoly powers, this inefficiency might be reflected simply in higher prices rather than financial losses. This also implies a more limited choice for consumers.

(b) **Planning costs** Economic management and the administration of government-sponsored production involves the use of scarce resources which might other- wise be used directly in the production of goods and services. There is also a danger that such administration develops a *bureaucracy* which decreases the efficiency of decision-making and of the productive process. Addition- ally, there is considerable controversy over the efficacy of government management of the economy: planning is a complex activity and many variables are outside the govern- ment's control. Some economists believe that misguided attempts at demand management have had a destabilizing effect on economic activity.

Appendix: Policy and Analysis

It is inappropriate in a book such as this to embark on a lengthy consideration of the methodology of the subject, but one aspect needs mention since it is so often a cause of misunderstanding.

The media present us daily with 'economic commentators' who are very liberal with advice on what the government *should* or *should not* do to resolve whatever particular aspect of the problem of scarcity is causing concern at the time. These policy prescriptions are usually based on an analysis both of what causes the problem and of the predicted effects of certain measures.

As an academic discipline, economics is concerned with analysis, but not with policy prescription. The economist can analyse the contributory causes of a particular problem and attempt to predict the consequences of particular policy measures determined by the government. It is, however, for the government to choose its objectives and to select its preferred measures, since these are based on political priorities and value judgements, for which there is no objective economic test of validity.

Of course, as a citizen, the person who has a grounding in economics may have strong personal views on appropriate economic policies, but these reflect a personal scale of priorities rather than any absolute scale. Thus, economics is traditionally described as a **positive science**, based on statements which can be tested by appeal to the facts.

Chapter 2

National Income

Definition National income is the total annual value of the flow of factor incomes accruing to the residents of a country, resulting from the production of goods and the provision of services.

There are three basic measures:

Gross Domestic Product (GDP) Incomes resulting from producing goods and services in the home economy.

Gross National Product (GNP) Includes GDP plus incomes to home residents from assets owned abroad, less the corresponding payments by residents to foreigners. This adjustment is known as 'net property income from abroad'.

Net National Product (NNP) In this measure a deduction is made from GNP for the consumption of capital ('depreciation') resulting from the year's productive activity. In official statistics, this figure is termed *the* National Income, although economists generally use GNP as a more appropriate measure of the current level of economic activity.

The adjustments may be summarized thus:

	£ million
Gross domestic product at factor cost	193 488
plus Net property income from abroad	−38
Gross national product at factor cost	193 450
less Capital consumption	27 045
National income (i.e. net national product)	166 405

Table 1. U.K. National Income 1980 (£ million) (Source: *National Income and Expenditure 1981*, HMSO)

MEASUREMENT OF NATIONAL INCOME

The national income accounts are based on an important identity between income output and expenditure. If a firm sells a car for £5000, it is apparent that the value of its output must be equal to the amount spent by the buyer to purchase the car. The revenue of the firm is (as was demonstrated in the previous chapter) equal to the sum of factor payments made in order to acquire the resources used to produce the car (remembering that the firm's profits are a factor payment). This identity can be most clearly seen from the diagram of the price system on page 12. In any real economy there will be various complications, such as accounting for government economic activity and international trade, but with the proper adjustments the identity holds true:

National income ≡ National output ≡ National expenditure

In measuring national income, there are five basic points to keep in mind:

1. Consistency It may be necessary to make adjustments to ensure consistency between the measures. For example, if a firm builds up its stocks during one year, this would show in the production and income accounts, but would not appear in the expenditure account (since the goods have not yet been bought). Therefore, it is necessary to include 'the value of the physical increase in stocks and work in progress' of firms within the expenditure account to achieve consistency between the measures.

2. Double-counting It is necessary to avoid counting the same activity more than once within the same account. For example, many firms produce goods which become the input of other firms (e.g. raw materials and machines) and become embodied in the value of those firms' outputs. Thus, only the *value added* to production by each firm is counted.

3. Transfer payments Another example of double-counting arises where payments are made which are not in return for the provision of factor services ('transfer payments'), e.g. state welfare payments. As these payments are transfers of income from one group to another (and since incomes are measured before tax), these transfers must be excluded as they do not form part of the value of the year's productive activity. The general criterion is that only incomes received in return for the provision of factor services should be included.

4. Foreign trade The purpose of the accounts is to measure economic activity within a country. Since imported goods do not represent domestic production or the payment of factor incomes to domestic residents, their value must be excluded. By the same argument, the value of exported goods must be included, since they do represent domestic production and income payments. This, therefore, is another example of the need to ensure consistency between the measures.

5. Accuracy For reasons often connected with tax avoidance or concealing other nefarious activities from the authorities, certain elements of income, production and expenditure will be concealed. This will result in some inconsistency between the accounts. For example, a 'pirate' video operator is producing a service from which he gains an income, but neither is recorded. However, he will spend at least part of this income, which will be recorded in the national income accounts.

The Expenditure Method
The expenditure account totals the spending of consumers, firms, the government and foreigners on domestically produced goods and services during a year. As seen above, imports are excluded and the value of the physical increase in stocks and work in progress is added (since this represents new production). Similarly, transfer payments by the government are excluded from 'general government final consumption'.

Domestic expenditure, U.K. 1980

(£ million)

Consumers' expenditure	135403
General government final consumption	48337
Gross domestic fixed capital formation	40050
Value of physical increase in stocks and work in progress	−3596
Total domestic expenditure at market prices	220194
Exports of goods and services	63198
Total final expenditure	283392
less Imports of goods and services	57832
Gross domestic product at market prices	225560
less Taxes on expenditure	37287
plus Subsidies	5215
Gross domestic product at factor cost	193488

Table 2. U.K. Domestic Expenditure (Source: *Ibid,* Table 1.1)

The figures are collected from a variety of sources, such as the national food survey, H.M. Customs and Excise, inquiries by the Department of Trade and Industry, the family expenditure survey and the Inland Revenue. Indeed, the number of sources increases the likelihood of double-counting or omissions. There are also problems related to timing of expenditure, particularly where long-term capital projects are involved.

As far as possible, transactions are recorded at the time when the expenditure is incurred, and at the market price actually paid. Because of indirect taxes, market prices may be higher than the factor cost of production (and hence the value of factor incomes created), so that expenditure taxes must be deducted for consistency with the other measures (and by the same argument, subsidies must be added). This factor cost adjustment is shown in Table 2.

The Income Method
This measure accounts for the incomes (before tax) of all individuals and firms in the economy during a year, plus the trading surplus of the public sector (see Table 3).

One or two points in the income table require clarification:

Stock appreciation Changes in the *value* of stocks (as opposed to increases in the physical *volume* of stocks) do not represent new productive activity and are therefore deducted for consistency with the other measures.

Transfer payments As all incomes are 'gross' (i.e. before tax), transfer payments must be excluded to avoid double-counting (see page 20).

GNP by category of income, U.K. 1980

(£ million)

Income from employment	137083
Income from self-employment	18394
Gross trading profits of companies	24979
Gross trading surplus of public corporations	6015
Gross trading surplus of general government enterprises	170
Rent	13231
Imputed charge for consumption of non-trading capital	2138
Total domestic income	202010
less Stock appreciation	6477
Gross domestic product (income-based)	195533
Residual error	−2045
Gross domestic product (expenditure-based)	193488

Table 3. U.K. National Income (Source: *Ibid,* Table 1.2)

Much of the information in the income account is derived from Inland Revenue tax statistics together with the accounts of central and local government and the public corporations. As has been mentioned, certain economic activities are likely to be unrecorded, giving rise to what is known as the 'hidden' or 'black' economy (see page 26).

The Product (or Output) Method
This method accounts for the annual value-added of different industries in the production of goods and services.

Gross domestic product by industry, U.K. 1980

(£ million)

Agriculture, forestry and fishing	4296
Petroleum and natural gas	7649
Other mining and quarrying	3222
Manufacturing	48060
Construction	13025
Gas, electricity and water	5803
Transport	10084
Communication	5326
Distributive trades	19328
Insurance, banking, finance and business services	18288
Ownership of dwellings	11996
Professional and scientific services	25467
Miscellaneous services	18734
Public administration and defence	13987
Total	205265
Adjustment for financial services	−9732
Residual error	−2045
Gross domestic product at factor cost	193488

Table 4. U.K. Domestic Product (Source: *Ibid,* Table 1.9)

The 'adjustment for financial services' represents net interest receipts, which is excluded to avoid double-counting. Similarly, we have noted that only the value added to production by each industry is counted, which avoids double-counting of the output of other industries or the inclusion of imported components (which are not a part of *domestic* output). Other problems include estimating the value of payments in kind and the value of output of workers with no tangible product (e.g. teachers). The provision of factor services for which no income is paid (e.g. do-it-yourself work, housewives) is excluded from the accounts.

The main sources of information for these statistics are the annual census of production and surveys by individual government departments.

USES OF NATIONAL INCOME STATISTICS

The national income accounts as presented above are in a convenient summary form. The accounts are published annually in the HMSO publication, *National Income and Expenditure,* known widely as 'the Blue Book' (because of the colour of its covers). The Blue Book also contains more detailed analysis of the various components of national income, and shows changes over time (usually between 10 and 20 years) as well as presenting the statistics in different forms. In many instances, the more detailed figures are of greater use in business applications. In every case, the limitations of the statistics and the notes on the accounts must be carefully considered. The Central Statistical Office publishes *The National Accounts : A Short Guide* (Studies in Official Statistics No. 36, HMSO) which is recommended.

Some indication of the range of information (and its applications) which can be derived from the national accounts is given below, but this is by no means a comprehensive list.

1. Trends in industrial production One way of analysing the changing structure of the economy is to use index numbers of industrial production at constant factor cost (Table 2.4 in the Blue Book). The index compares production of different industries over time.

2. Trends in consumer expenditure The national accounts give fairly detailed statistics on consumers' expenditure over time for specified product groups. Spending on any one item might be compared with, for example, total expenditure, changes in personal disposable income or changes in national income.

3. Changes in the distribution of income Table 3 shows the *'functional distribution of income'*, i.e. how national income is divided between the different factor services. Changes in this share over time may be useful indicators to different types of business, e.g. the capital goods industry might expect a rise in demand for their products if the gross trading profits of companies was seen to rise.

Other available information

Having seen that some information of value to the business sector can be gathered from the national income accounts, it should not be assumed that these are the most useful source. Their usefulness is limited by the time-lag (they do not appear until September of the following year) and by the lack of information relating to sub-groups within industrial sectors. Thus, businessmen may find monthly and quarterly estimates far more useful (and more immediate), or may use more detailed sources on a wider range of variables with more specific reference to their particular activities.

For example, the *Monthly Digest of Statistics* (also published by the Central Statistical Office) not only provides quarterly estimates of national income and expenditure statistics, but much more detailed figures on production, sales, costs and prices in different industries.

However, wider economic implications can be drawn from the national income statistics, and it is this aspect of the annual accounts which is often of primary interest to the economist. The list of uses of the national income statistics can therefore be extended as shown below.

4. Economic growth and the standard of living

Once the figures are adjusted for (a) changes in the price level, and (b) changes in the size of population, it is possible to make some comparison of economic activity over time. The figure used is real national income per head, and the rate of change of this figure from year to year is the conventional measure of 'economic growth'.

Economic growth is generally considered desirable as it *implies* the availability of more goods and services per person, and hence a higher material standard of living: expressed simply, the average person would be considered to be better off. The table below shows how dubious this assertion can be.

	1975	1976	1977	1978	1979	1980
Annual per capita growth of:						
Gross domestic product (%)						
	−0.6	+3.9	+1.1	+2.9	+0.7	−1.8
Personal disposable income (%)						
	−1.6	−0.6*	−1.7	+8.4	+6.2	+1.8
Consumers' expenditure (%)						
	−0.6	+0.3	−0.5	+6.0	+4.6	+0.6

Table 5. (Source: adapted from *Economic Trends,* September 1981, p.14, HMSO)

Table 5 demonstrates that there can be a substantial difference between the rate of growth of national income per head and either *per capita* consumers' expenditure or personal disposable income, both of which seem more likely to indicate material welfare in the household sector than national income does.

The rate of economic growth derived from national income statistics may give an inaccurate impression of changes in material welfare because:

(a) The figure is a broad average, and takes no account of the effect of changes in the distribution of income.

(b) No account is taken of changes in the composition of national income which may affect the proportion of income which is available to domestic consumers to improve their living standards, e.g. increased production of producer durables or goods for export will increase national income but will not *at that time* necessarily increase the goods and services available to consumers.

(c) The figure is purely quantitative, and takes no account of changes in the *quality* of the goods and services produced which might (for example) be improved by technological progress. In 1980, for example, the production of an electronic calculator may have represented £5 added to national output, whereas in 1970 the equivalent article may have accounted for £100 of output.

(d) The accuracy of the statistics may vary over time.

Moreover, increases in material welfare are not the only consideration in estimating changes in the average standard of living, if this is taken in the broader sense of meaning 'well-being'. We also need to take into account:

(e) Externalities The increased production of goods and services may bring with it adverse side-effects, such as increased pollution or congestion, or beneficial side-effects, such as decreased stress, control of diseases and so forth. Having a 'bigger cake' is one thing, but deriving increased well-being from that opportunity is another.

(f) The quality of life Real national income per head may be increased simply by substituting work for leisure, but this does not necessarily mean that the average person will feel better off. Much depends on the relative valuation of leisure time, and the opportunities which become available to derive benefit from it.

5. International comparison

The final use of national income statistics to be considered relates to making comparisons of different countries' growth rates and hence, by implication, of their relative living standards. The most obvious objection here is that the criticisms of the domestic use of the statistics for this purpose apply equally (if not more) when different countries are compared. For example, one country may devote more of its resources to expanding the capital base or to the provision of exports, or its statistics may be less accurate, or it may incur more adverse side-effects when compared with another country. There are some additional problems specific to international comparison:

(a) Exchange rates In order to compare two countries' income statistics, it is necessary to convert them into a common currency using exchange rates. However, exchange rates are influenced by the types of good most commonly traded, differences in domestic inflation and interest rates, government intervention, speculation and so forth. Consequently, whereas an identical car may be produced in both countries, its value in terms of national output may be quite different when converted via exchange rate. In other words, the exchange rate will not necessarily reflect the relative purchasing powers of income in the different countries.

(b) Statistical convention Different criteria may be applied as to what items should be included or excluded.

(c) Different needs The well-being of people will be related to the degree to which identified needs are satisfied. Since these may be influenced by such diverse factors as culture and climate, which vary considerably between nations, national income statistics alone are an inadequate means of comparing relative well-being.

Summary

None of this is intended to suggest that national income statistics are useless. What is suggested is that in some cases there will be other, more appropriate, statistics available for a given purpose; that when the figures are used for comparison over time, or between countries, some caution must be exercised; and that other information may be useful, both in terms of the composition of the statistics and of other indicators of living standards (such as infant mortality rates, calorific intake, working hours, atmospheric pollution and so forth).

THE HIDDEN (OR 'BLACK') ECONOMY

We referred above to economic activity which tends not to be measured in official accounts. The existence and scale of the 'hidden economy' has attracted considerable economic interest in recent years. It may take many different forms and constitutes a different proportion of total economic activity in different countries.

1. Unemployed earners These are people who, despite being registered as unemployed and claiming state benefits, are actually earning an income which is not declared to the authorities. A small proportion of these are in fact employed on a regular full-time basis or (more commonly) are engaged in commercial activities on their own behalf. A more significant problem, quantitatively perhaps, are those genuinely seeking full-time employment who fail to declare casual earnings (which are deductible from state benefits).

2. Moonlighting About 3% of the U.K. workforce are reckoned to have regular employment in second jobs (i.e. in addition to their main employment). This, of course, in itself does not contribute to the black economy: it is only where such employment is not declared for tax purposes that the activity is hidden from the national income accounts. Moonlighting has increased in recent years because of decreased working hours in formal jobs, better working conditions and the financial pressures on households of decreased formal economic activity during prolonged depression in the 1970s.

3. 'Working the fiddle' This phrase is applied to a variety of sources of income which are undeclared. There are, for example, various forms of pilfering which range from stealing business property, short-changing customers and under-delivery, to 'expert fiddles' which trade on the technical ignorance of customers of the services they pay for.

4. Payments in cash or kind These can include other aspects of 'working the fiddle'. For example, employees in service industries may engage in private transactions for cash payment during their normal working hours (often using their employer's materials and equipment). Alternatively, cash 'gratuities' may mysteriously decrease waiting times or make previously unavailable spare parts become available.

Since cash payment is difficult to trace, it may be encouraged by tradesmen in domestic services (particularly those who are self-employed) as a means of concealing income from the authorities. Such activities have undoubtedly increased in recent years, partly as a result of the decline in formal economic activity and the low capital requirement to form a business in the service sector, and also because of the increased demand for such services resulting from the increased accumulation of consumer durable goods (which require servicing).

Payments in kind are forms of income, and as such are subject to income tax. However, they are as difficult to trace as cash transactions, so that the decorator who paints his butcher's house in return for a re-stocked freezer may be tempted to conceal the fact from the Inland Revenue. There is some evidence to suggest that, especially where the cost of borrowing money is high, barter transactions of this type have become increasingly common.

5. Illegitimate business expenses Legitimate business expenses can be off-set against tax liability. However, it is often difficult to distinguish between business and personal expenditure. Receipts of 'perks' are often personal income thinly disguised as business expenses. This may be a particular problem in the case of the self-employed, where there are obvious tax benefits from receiving income in this concealed form.

Significance of the hidden economy
Because it is concealed, it is difficult to quantify the importance of the hidden economic activity described above. The 'guestimate' for the U.K. economy is usually quoted at 7.5% of national income, i.e. about £13bn, representing something in the region of £4bn in lost tax revenue. There is some evidence that hidden activity has grown as formal

activity has suffered during the 1970s, although this by no means suggests that the depression is purely a statistical phenomenon.

One strand of evidence is the divergence between expenditure and income. At the national level, there has been a tendency for the expenditure figure for national income to exceed the income figure by a greater amount, which might suggest increased hidden activity as expenditure is more difficult to conceal than income. At the household level, the self-employed, who have greater opportunity to conceal activity perhaps, do spend a greater proportion of their declared income than other groups (which suggests that their declared income may be under-stated).

A final pointer to the growth of the hidden economy is the increase in demand for large denomination notes, which may be partly accounted for by a growth in cash transactions in the hidden economy.

It is sometimes argued that activity in the hidden economy results from excessive taxation but countries with smaller tax burdens than the U.K. are thought to have hidden economies at least as great. The U.S.A.'s black economy has been estimated at 10% of national income, for example. In some other countries, such as Italy, hidden economic activity is of even larger dimensions.

The hidden economy may represent an economic problem in that, by under-stating formal economic activity, it may cause government economic policy (e.g. on unemployment) to be misguided. It certainly means that the formal economy bears a greater tax burden than would otherwise be necessary to maintain the same level of government expenditure. Moreover, if due tax revenue was derived from the hidden economy, the need for the government to borrow would be reduced, which would tend to lower interest rates with benefit to industry in the formal economy, encouraging increased investment and employment.

Apart from the moral and fiscal issues involved, there are obvious benefits from a thriving black economy. Since part of the incomes are spent and represent demand for business in the formal economy, hidden economic activity does help to maintain employment and output. The fact that resources which might otherwise be unemployed are put to work in the black economy also suggests that the economy is operating more efficiently than it otherwise would. It could be argued that if black economy transactions occur they must provide mutual benefit for both buyer and seller, and presumably a benefit greater than could be achieved within the formal economy (or else the transaction would occur in the formal economy).

This is not intended to justify illegal activity. Indeed, the benefits of bringing such activity back within the formal economy seem likely to outweigh the costs of detection.

NATIONAL INCOME DETERMINATION

This section is concerned with the factors which determine the level of national income in an economy in the short run. The main principles can be demonstrated from a simple model of the circular flow of income, in which there is no foreign trade (i.e. a 'closed economy') or government economic activity. This is similar to the price system diagram on page 12, except that we now allow for savings by firms and households, and for investment by the business sector. In the diagram below, we show savings (S) as a single *leakage* from the economy, and investment (I) as an *injection* (i.e. another form of demand for domestically produced goods and services).

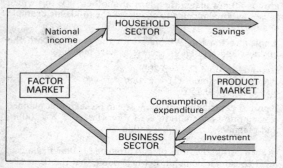

Figure 2. Simple model of the circular flow of income

This is a simple representation of the model put forward by John Maynard Keynes (1883–1946) whose '*General Theory of Employment, Interest and Money*' (1936) has dominated macroeconomic theory for most of the post-war period. An important part of the theory is that households' consumption expenditure (C) and saving plans are dependent on the level of national income: Keynes used the term '*propensity*', meaning a psychological inclination to do something.

Definitions

The **average propensity to consume** (apc) is the proportion of income which households plan to spend on consumer goods and services.

The **marginal propensity to consume** (mpc) is the proportion of a *change* in income which households plan to spend.

The **average propensity to save** (aps) is the proportion of disposable income which households plan not to spend.

The **marginal propensity to save** (mps) is the proportion of a *change* in disposable income which households plan not to spend.

Using the symbols 'Y' for national income, and 'Δ' (delta) for 'a change in', we can write these definitions as:

$$apc = \frac{C}{Y} \quad mpc = \frac{\Delta C}{\Delta Y} \quad aps = \frac{S}{Y} \quad mps = \frac{\Delta S}{\Delta Y}$$

Planned investment (I) is said to be *'autonomous'*, i.e. it does not depend on the level of national income.

National income equilibrium

It is important to distinguish between the *planned* levels of consumption, savings and investment, and the *realized* (or 'actual') values of these variables. Since decisions are made by different 'actors', it is quite likely that the plans of one group will not match the plans of another: it is this which causes national income to change as the following example demonstrates.

1. Initial situation We start with the plans of both the business and household sectors exactly matching.

National income (Y) = £200bn
Planned Investment (I) = £50bn
apc = mpc = 0.75Y

Figure 3 depicts this situation. It can be seen that planned consumption expenditure is £150bn (i.e. 0.75 × £200bn) and planned savings equal £50bn.

In each period the firms plan to produce £150bn of goods to meet consumer demand. Let us assume that the firms also plan to increase their stocks of consumer goods (as part of their investment programme) by £10bn. The remaining £40bn is spent on increasing the capital stock and buying raw materials. So, the firms' total production during each period is £160bn of consumer goods (£10bn of which are intended to increase their stocks).

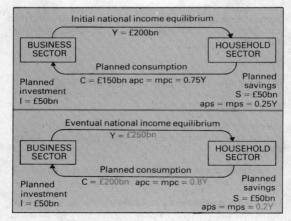

Figure 3. Changes in national income equilibrium

As long as the plans of all the actors are unchanged, it can be seen that the flow will continue unaltered from one time period to the next.

2. Disequilibrium Now we can observe what happens if one group changes its plans. We assume that planned consumption rises to 0.8Y (and consequently planned savings fall to 0.2Y).

In the first instance, savings will fall to £40bn and consumption expenditure will rise to £160bn (i.e. 0.8 × £200bn). This means that the firms will have sold £10bn more of consumer goods than they planned, and will therefore have failed in their plans to increase their stocks by £10bn. Thus, realized savings (£40bn) equal planned savings (0.2Y), but realized investment (£40bn) is less than planned investment (£50bn) because of the failure to increase stocks as planned.

This demonstrates that *realized* savings will always equal *realized* investment in the simple model. But what matters most is the fact that *planned* investment is greater than *planned* savings. This is important because it will prompt the firms to change their policy.

3. Eventual equilibrium If the firms assume that they will continue to sell the new level of £160bn of goods to consumers each period, they are likely to increase their production by £10bn (to £170bn per period) in an attempt to achieve the planned increase in their stocks. This increased production represents incomes (in the form of rent, interest and profits as well as wages), and so national income will rise by £10bn.

However, we know that four-fifths of this increase in income will be consumed (mpc = 0.8 ΔY), so that the firms' stocks will actually only increase by £2bn. Thus we would expect the firms to increase their production again (by £8bn this time), and so the process continues.

Each period, the firms will increase their production until they achieve their planned increase in stocks. This will occur when income has risen to £250bn, at which time planned savings will equal £50bn (0.2Y) which matches with the firms' investment plans. Equilibrium has then been restored: there is no incentive for firms to change their output, as their plans are now realized.

We can deduce three important points about national income determination (in the simple model) from this example:

(a) National income equilibrium occurs where planned savings and planned investment are equal.
(b) In equilibrium, aggregate demand (planned C + planned I) is equal to the level of national income.
(c) An initial change in aggregate demand results in a

much greater eventual change in national income. In our example, planned consumption increased initially by £10bn, causing an eventual change in national income of £50bn. This is known as the **multiplier effect**.

The final equilibrium is shown in the lower half of Figure 3, with the changes printed in red. However, this circular flow presentation is a relatively cumbersome way of showing the effects of changes in demand, and so economists generally represent such ideas by a means of a graph based on the conclusions we derived from our simple example.

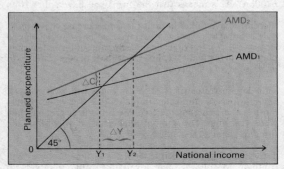

Figure 4. National income determination

The 'secret' to understanding the graph is our second conclusion from the numerical example. The 45° line connects all the points at which **aggregate monetary demand** (AMD), or total planned expenditure by firms and households (C+I), is equal to the level of national income. Thus, the equilibrium level of national income is where a line showing planned expenditure at every level of income (marked as AMD in Figure 4) crosses the 45° line.

Thus, in Figure 4, with the initial level of planned expenditure at AMD_1, national income is in equilibrium at Y_1.

The AMD function, in the simple model, has two elements: planned consumption and planned investment. As planned investment is constant (whatever the level of national income), a change in investment plans would cause a *parallel* shift of the AMD function. Planned consumption, on the other hand, depends on the level of national income: it rises as national income rises, which accounts for the slope of the AMD function. So, if (as in our example) the propensity to consume changes, then the *slope* of the AMD function changes.

Figure 4, therefore, shows the effect of a change in planned consumption. Initially, consumption expenditure rises by ΔC, which leads to a new equilibrium at Y_2; again, we note that national income has risen by a greater amount than the initial increase in aggregate demand.

Full model of income determination

For the purpose of explanation we have considered an economy with only one 'leakage' (savings) from the circular flow, and only one injection (investment). The full model of income determination takes into account two additional leakages: taxation (T) and imports (M); and two more injections: government spending (G) and exports (X).

Spending on imports is considered a leakage since the goods which are bought do not represent domestic output nor the creation of factor incomes in the home economy. On the other hand, exported goods are produced in the home economy and do create domestic factor incomes, so that expenditure by foreigners on our goods is a part of the home economy's aggregate demand.

In just the same way as for the simple model, we can express the equilibrium condition as:

Total planned leakages (L) = Total planned injections (J)

or, $T + S + M = G + I + X$

It should be noted that although taxes are obviously connected with government expenditure, and savings with investment, and imports with exports, the equilibrium condition is that *total* planned leakages must equal *total* planned injections, and *not* that each individual pair should be exactly matched.

We also found in the simple model that the economy was in equilibrium where national income was equal to aggregate demand. In the full model, aggregate monetary demand will comprise planned consumption (excluding indirect taxes and spending on imports) plus planned injections (investment, government spending and exports). The equilibrium diagram in Figure 4 remains exactly the same (although AMD now has more elements).

Each of the injections is assumed to be autonomous. Thus, an increase in exports, for example, will cause a parallel upward shift in the AMD function, raising the level of national income by a greater amount: the multiplier effect.

THE MULTIPLIER

Definition The multiplier is the number by which an initial change in aggregate monetary demand must be multiplied to find the eventual change in national income which results.

Using our previous example, the initial rise in aggregate monetary demand was £10bn and the eventual change in national income was £50bn, so that the value of the multiplier was 5.

The multiplier effect results from a devastatingly simple but dramatically significant observation: *one person's expenditure is another person's income.* It is no exaggeration to say that Keynesian economics is based on this simple fact. Expenditure is the culminating act of a cycle of production and income creation.

When a man buys a suit at the local department store for £60, the whole of that £60 represents factor incomes for the people involved in the production and distribution of the suit. Most obviously this will include the wages of the workers who made and distributed the suit, but it will also include an element of profit for the shareholders in the manufacturing firm and the department store, as well as payments of interest and rent on the capital and property used to make and distribute the suit.

Since all factor services are owned in the household sector, one person's expenditure of £60 will create incomes totalling £60 for a large number of others. Part of this £60 will be taken in taxes, saved or spent on imported goods (i.e. leaked from the circular flow), but the remainder will be spent on domestically produced goods and services, creating new incomes, part of which will be spent, and so on. The greater the proportion of income which is spent on domestically produced goods and services, the greater will be the multiplier effect.

Numerical value of the multiplier

By definition, a change in planned leakages (ΔL) will be equal to the change in national income (ΔY) multiplied by the marginal rate of leakage (mrl):

$$\Delta L = mrl(\Delta Y)$$

In equilibrium, planned leakages (L) are equal to planned injections (J), so ΔL must equal ΔJ for equilibrium to be restored. Thus, by substitution, we can write:

$$\Delta J = mrl(\Delta Y)$$

We can rewrite this equation as:

$$\frac{\Delta Y}{\Delta J} = \frac{1}{mrl}$$

Since $\Delta Y/\Delta J$ is the ratio of the change in income to the change in planned injections, $1/mrl$ is the numerical value of the multiplier. This can be checked from our previous numerical example, where $\Delta Y = £250bn$, $\Delta J = £50bn$ and $mrl = 0.2$. (For ΔJ we can substitute ΔAMD.) Since that part of income which does not leak from the circular flow is consumption expenditure, we can express the multiplier (k) in several different forms:

$$k = \frac{\Delta Y}{\Delta AMD} = \frac{1}{mrl} = \frac{1}{1-mpc}$$

The importance of the multiplier

At first sight, the income determination model and the multiplier effect may seem rather remote from the practical world of the businessman. In fact, nothing could be further from the truth, since the business sector is directly affected by the general level of activity in the economy.

Insofar as increased income reflects increased output, the multiplier effect demonstrates the factors which influence output and demand, and hence employment and profits. If the level of economic activity falls, firms will need to adjust their production and marketing strategies accordingly. In some industries, the responsiveness of the quantity demanded to changes in income *(income elasticity of demand)* may be particularly high, which would require more radical changes of strategy.

The multiplier effect can also be used to demonstrate the effects of government expenditure programmes. For example, when the government decides to build a new motorway, the effects on employment and production in related sectors, such as the construction and civil engineering industries, are self-evident. What the multiplier highlights is the 'knock-on' effects of this increase in production. Since new incomes are created for people providing the factor services used in building the motorway, and given that part of these incomes will be spent on domestically produced goods and services, increased demand (and hence output and employment) will be experienced in industries totally unconnected with the construction industry. Indeed, the effect is often likened to throwing a stone into the centre of a pond, causing ripples which eventually spread throughout the water.

The multiplier also demonstrates the importance of firms' investment plans and export achievements. Since these have a much wider impact than their initial purpose, governments may take measures to encourage such aspects of business activity (although there may be other contributory reasons for such policies, such as the balance of payments).

Finally, knowledge of the multiplier gives the government a quantitative guide in assessing the consequences of those of its actions which affect the level of aggregate demand. Potentially, since the government can directly influence the level of aggregate demand by changing the rates of taxation or the level of its planned expenditure, the government could use the multiplier effect to control the level of aggregate demand so that resources in the economy are fully employed (without 'over-heating' the economy by causing demand to exceed the business sector's capacity to produce). However, this 'fine-tuning' of the economy is a complex task and is fraught with problems, as is explained in the next chapter.

Chapter 3

Government Intervention

In Chapter 1, the main reasons for government intervention were summarized as follows:

1. Provision of merit goods.
2. Payments of welfare benefits.
3. Control of production where natural monopoly exists.
4. Provision of social capital (including public goods).
5. To take account of the effects of externalities.
6. Provision of aid for industry.
7. Management of the economy.

In addition, it was noted that governments would seek to reduce 'imperfections' in the private sector of the economy by, for example, control of monopolies and restrictive practices or reduction of the immobility of factors.

Broadly speaking, we can divide government intervention between its effects on the economy as a whole ('macro-economic effects') and its effects on individual parts of the economy, such as individual firms or consumers (i.e. its 'microeconomic effects'). In this chapter we are primarily concerned with the macroeconomic effects of government intervention, and specifically with the problems of demand management, fiscal policy and public finance.

DEMAND MANAGEMENT

The need for governments to intervene to influence the overall level of economic activity ('demand management') arises from observed tendencies for the level of activity to fluctuate over time, known as the *business cycle*. That is, there are deviations above and below the long-term growth trend of the economy which may, for example, be measured with reference to national income, consumers' expenditure, fixed investment, stock-building and unemployment.

Business cycles

The existence of business cycles means that at certain times the economy will be operating with spare capacity, with scarce resources either unemployed or under-employed. At other times parts of the economy will be 'over-heated', so that bottlenecks in the production process occur. A simplified model of the business cycle is given in Figure 5, which shows deviations of economic activity (having removed the long-term growth trend).

One simplified explanation of the existence of business cycles involves the multiplier effect. Starting at the peak of the cycle, a fall in aggregate demand would cause a multiple decrease in national income, launching the economy into the recession phase. As demand falls, firms may decrease their planned investment (since they do not need to increase their productive capacity), which would accelerate the fall in national income. However, the demand for some firms (specifically those with a low income elasticity of demand for their products) will not fall as quickly as others, so that eventually they will need to invest to maintain output at the required level. This gives an impetus to demand (as incomes rise in the capital goods industry) which, through the multiplier, causes national income to rise again. At first, economic activity may pick up quickly as unused capacity is taken up. The sharp rise in demand is likely to require increased investment in order to expand capacity (which causes an exaggerated increased demand in the capital goods industry, known as the **'accelerator effect'**). Eventually, as bottlenecks arise in the supply of factors, the rate of growth of output will slow down. This causes the accelerator effect to go into reverse: demand in the capital goods industry actually *decreases* as the rate of growth of consumer demand slows down. As incomes and output in the capital goods industry decline, the downward multiplier effect operates again, and the cycle is complete.

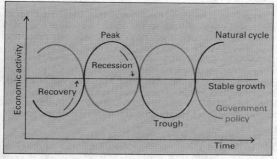

Figure 5. The business cycle

Governments seek to remove (or reduce) these cyclical deviations because of the economic and social problems they are likely to cause. During a depression, resources are under-employed and real incomes tend to fall. In human terms, mass unemployment might persist over a long period in the absence of government intervention: not only a waste of scarce resources, but a significant social problem representing frustration, humiliation and financial stringency. On the other hand, the 'boom' period tends to be associated with problems such as rising inflation and (if increased imports satisfy excess domestic demand) balance of payments crises.

Figure 5 shows the policy cycle which would be necessary to remove cyclical fluctuations. During the boom period, the government would need to act to depress aggregate demand, while during the recession phase it would need to boost demand. In terms of our national income determination model, the government should be able to influence the level of aggregate demand either directly, by controlling G and T, or indirectly, by influencing savings, investment and foreign trade. These 'fine-tuning' strategies are demonstrated in Figure 6.

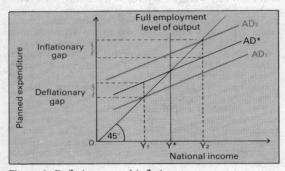

Figure 6. Deflationary and inflationary gaps

The analysis is based on the premise that, in the short term, there is a physical limit to the level of economic activity which can be achieved without over-heating the economy. This is termed 'the full employment level of output', which is rather misleading since it allows for a certain level of unemployment to facilitate factor mobility. In principle, national income equilibrium at the full employment level of output (which would be achieved with a level of aggregate demand AD*) would permit optimum utilization of resources without inflation or involuntary unemployment.

If the level of aggregate demand was below AD*, for example at AD₁ in the diagram, national income equilibrium would be below the full employment level of output at Y₁. It was the observation that an *equilibrium* below full employment could persist which distinguishes Keynesian theory from that of the classical economists. The latter argued that full employment was the 'natural' state of the economy, and that national income would always revert automatically to the full employment level in the long run. Keynes's famed retort to this, in view of the lengthy and severe depression of the 1930s, was that 'in the long run we are all dead'.

From the diagram it can be seen that if national income is in equilibrium at Y₁, there would need to be an initial increase in aggregate demand shown by the vertical distance between AD₁ and AD* to achieve (via the multiplier) full employment equilibrium. This distance is termed the **deflationary gap**: the amount by which aggregate demand is insufficient to achieve full employment equilibrium. In this case, the aim of government demand management policy would be to increase aggregate demand to the desired level, AD*.

On the other hand, the level of aggregate demand (expressed in monetary terms) might exceed the economy's productive capacity. For example, if aggregate monetary demand is equal to AD_2, national income equilibrium occurs at Y_2. Since, by definition, the physical limit to output is Y^*, any increase in income beyond this level must represent increased prices and incomes rather than increased production or employment.

In this case, the government would need to act to remove the **inflationary gap**: the amount by which aggregate monetary demand exceeds the level necessary to achieve full employment equilibrium. Again, because of the multiplier effect, the necessary decrease in aggregate demand will be smaller than the eventual change in national income which results.

Any government has a range of possible policy instruments available to it which can be used both to influence the general level of economic activity and to discriminate between different aspects and sectors of the economy. These can be classified as follows:

1. Fiscal policy The manipulation of government expenditure and taxation. In the Keynesian view this is the most direct means of influencing aggregate demand.

2. Monetary policy This involves controlling the supply of money in the economy and the cost of borrowing (i.e. interest rates).

3. Direct and institutional controls These are policies directed to specific aspects of an economic problem, for example, import controls in the face of a balance of payments crisis, or the use of the Monopolies and Mergers Commission to avert unfair competition.

In this chapter we are primarily concerned with fiscal policy, although we shall need to consider the degree to which this interacts with monetary policy. In the next chapter, we shall consider specific policy objectives and the alternative measures which might be appropriate to achieve them.

Problems of demand management

The discussion of the principles of demand management so far may have made it seem a relatively simple matter. This, quite obviously, is not the case. The main difficulties can be classified as follows:

1. Information problems In order to know what action is appropriate, the government depends on statistical information about the key economic indicators. There is obviously a *time-lag* involved both in the collection of data and its interpretation. Moreover, the *accuracy* of provisional estimates can be dubious.

2. Timing problems Apart from the time-lag in collecting and interpreting data, delays will occur in determining the desired policy action, gaining parliamentary approval (where necessary), implementing the policy and its impact taking effect. Clearly, the actions which might have proved appropriate in the time period to which the data referred may be quite inappropriate by the time the policy takes effect. Hence, policy must be based on *forecasts* of the condition of the economy at the time when the policy takes effect. This, of course, reintroduces the problem of *accuracy*.

3. Quantitative problems Generally, it will not be too difficult to determine the direction of change in aggregate demand which is required, but from the practical viewpoint governments need to know the amount of change which is necessary. If the values of the multiplier and accelerator effects fluctuate over time, and if the economy is subject to external influences beyond the government's control, then given the problems already mentioned, estimating the precise quantitative degree of change is extraordinarily difficult.

4. Analytical problems Clearly, the government's demand management is only likely to be successful if it is based on a correct analysis of the causes of a given problem. In the next chapter the magnitude of this problem will become apparent.

5. Feedback problems Any policy actions which the government takes may adversely affect other policy objectives, e.g. attempts to decrease inflation may have the effect of increasing unemployment.

Notwithstanding these problems, the use of Keynesian demand management techniques in the post-war period has coincided with a reduction in the amplitude of cyclical fluctuations and a shortening of the duration of cycles. The average level of economic activity relative to full employment seems to have been consistently higher during this period. However, during the 1970s prolonged periods of depression, accompanied by relatively high levels of inflation and international payments crises, encouraged a growing doubt about the ability of governments to fine-tune the economy, and indeed about the wisdom of attempting to do so. Monetarist economists have argued that demand management techniques have, in the long term, tended to destabilize economies. This controversy is considered in more detail later in the chapter.

FISCAL POLICY

Fiscal policy can be defined as the actions of government to influence economic activity through the manipulation of taxation and government expenditure.

Automatic stabilizers There is a sense in which fiscal policy inevitably stabilizes the level of economic activity. For example, if unemployment rises, tax receipts will fall and government expenditure on welfare benefits will rise, other things being equal. This will result in aggregate demand falling less quickly than in the absence of government involvement in the economy. The government has not taken any deliberate action to achieve this effect: it occurs automatically once the change in activity occurs. By the same token, this aspect of fiscal policy clearly cannot prevent the change from occurring in the first place, which is the purpose of *discretionary* fiscal policy where the government deliberately changes tax rates or the level of its spending to alter the level of economic activity.

General government expenditure, U.K.

(£ million, current prices)	1970	1975	1980
Military defence	2460	5166	11388
External relations	331	672	2072
Roads and public lighting	807	1506	2302
Transport and communication	478	1507	1243
Employment services	128	477	1692
Other industry and trade	1603	3533	4075
Agriculture, forestry, fishing and food	398	1727	1589
Housing	1319	4459	7156
Other environmental services	854	2263	3828
Law and order[1]	521	1397	3280
Education	2532	6595	11886
National Health Service	1979	5134	11494
Personal social services	257	1001	2127
Social security benefits	3921	8905	22211
Other items	3308	7289	17377
TOTAL EXPENDITURE	20896	51631	103720
Index of total expenditure (1975 = 100)	40.5	100	201
Retail Price Index (1975 = 100)	54.2	100	196

Table 6. U.K. general government expenditure (Source: adapted from *National Income and Expenditure, 1981* HMSO, and *Economic Trends, September 1981,* HMSO) [1]includes police and prison service, Parliament and law courts.

It can be seen from the table that government expenditure grew rapidly between 1970 and 1975 (by roughly one-third in real terms) and much more slowly in the following five years (by less than 3% in real terms). The individual items reflect the reasons for intervention (such as the provision of merit goods, welfare payments, social capital and aid for industry) previously cited.

The massive total expenditure figure in the table (accounting for over 50% of GDP in 1980) overstates the government's claims on the national resources, since many of the items simply represent transfers of income (which the recipients will use to buy goods and services). Thus, the more appropriate figure is 'general government final consumption': spending on goods and services by central and local government. This figure amounted to roughly £50bn in 1980, representing about 25% of GDP.

Government expenditure and the business sector

Any element of government expenditure which is not spent on imported goods potentially increases the demand for the products of U.K. producers. This is equally true whether the expenditure is in the form of transfers of incomes to the household sector, subsidies and grants to the business sector, or direct government consumption. Any such increase in aggregate demand will have a multiplier effect, further increasing the demand for the output of the business sector. On the other hand such expenditure must be financed and, whether this is achieved by taxation or borrowing, there may be adverse effects on the business sector (which are discussed in the section below on *public finance*).

Government contracts may represent a large proportion of the business of some firms. For example, in the construction and civil engineering industries, planned expenditure on social capital directly affects output and employment. There have been situations where governments have sought to influence firms' behaviour with the lure (or threatened withdrawal) of government contracts, e.g. compliance with 'voluntary' incomes policies or regional policies. Indirectly, the pattern of government expenditure may affect a wider range of industries. For example, educational book publishers will experience decreased demand if current spending on education is reduced.

Thus, changes both in the overall level of government expenditure and in its distribution between different functions will affect the level of aggregate demand and the relative levels of demand between industries, with direct implications for firms' profitability.

Changes in public expenditure

It has been seen that, in principle, changes in government spending may be used to manage the level of demand within the economy. Indeed, certain elements of government spending change automatically as economic activity changes (e.g. welfare payments) or as the structure of population changes (e.g. educational provision).

As a means of fine-tuning, government spending is limited in its effect because:

1. Its full impact (particularly in the case of capital projects) may take a long time to feed through into aggregate demand.

2. There is a *ratchet effect:* once expenditure has increased it is difficult to reverse the policy.

3. Expenditure projects often represent long-term commitments which it may prove costly or inefficient to cancel before completion. (The cost of long-term capital projects has a habit of escalating out of all proportion to original estimates once the project commences, e.g. Concorde.)

4. Certain aspects of government spending are particularly sensitive politically.

Ignoring for the moment the problem of finance, increases in public expenditure are relatively easy to achieve, but expenditure cuts present a significant problem for the reasons already stated, such as statutory commitments, changes in population structure, long-term projects, social and political constraints, etc. Faced with an apparent choice between increasing taxes and cutting spending, however, the political choice often rests in favour of the latter. There are a number of tried and tested means of achieving this:

1. Sectoral discrimination Discretionary cuts in planned spending on those areas not subject to statutory commitment may be generalized, but more often are focused on the politically less sensitive budgets (depending on party preferences).

2. Capital expenditure Since expenditure cuts are usually related to planned future expenditure, postponing capital projects is one means of reducing spending without directly affecting existing provision. The scope for this is reduced the more frequently previous governments have resorted to this method: replacement investment cannot be postponed indefinitely.

3. Reducing waste Most governments find this easier to advocate than to achieve. Depending on how it is defined, the overall effect on the planning total is usually negligible.

4. Cash limits Over-spending by government departments and local authorities may be prevented by tighter cash controls.

5. Money illusion Budgets may be increased in money terms, but by less than the rate of inflation, in the hope that the cut in real terms is less apparent.

6. Manpower policy Governments may seek to impose wage increases below the 'norm' for its own employees, or to reduce manning levels. Union opposition is inevitable, and industrial disruption may result.

In practice, cuts in government expenditure in real terms are difficult to achieve. The problem is exacerbated by the cumulative effect of previous attempts at expenditure cutting, the need to maintain a core of essential services, and the fact that, to the extent that such cuts reduce aggregate demand and employment other elements of government spending (most notably welfare benefits) increase. This last problem is particularly relevant when, as in recent years, expenditure cuts occur in the context of an economy already operating with spare capacity.

PUBLIC FINANCE

The government needs to raise revenue to finance its spending plans (at central and local level), to service its debt, and to meet any deficits incurred by public corporations. The two main methods by which this public finance is raised are *taxation* and *borrowing*. There are, however, other forms of revenue, some of which need a brief mention:

1. National insurance contributions These are payments by employers and employees intended to cover expenditure on certain welfare payments. Amounting to nearly £14bn in 1980, they can be thought of as an alternative form of direct taxation. Indeed, the employers' surcharge has been criticized as a tax on employment, adding to production costs and discouraging employers from expanding their workforce.

2. Surplus of public corporations Public corporations can be used to affect central government expenditure (by avoiding the need for subsidies) or revenue (by transfer of any surplus). Thus, increasing revenue from public corporations, by raising prices where demand is relatively unresponsive, may be considered an alternative to increasing taxes.

3. Rent, interest and dividends Central and local government bodies receive interest on loans, as well as income from providing other factor services, e.g. rent on council houses. Receipts in these categories totalled nearly £7bn in 1980.

4. Sale of public assets The government may sell part of its assets to the private sector ('privatization'), e.g. floating shares in public corporations. Whilst this affords the short-term benefit of revenue from sales, the government obviously forgoes the future flow of profits which such assets would have provided. However, governments which wish to limit the scope of government intervention in industry may have motives other than finance for privatization.

Taxation
In the U.K., the direct and indirect taxes of central government account for about 70% of total tax receipts; the remainder comprises national insurance contributions (20%) and rates – a local property tax accounting for roughly 10% of total taxation. Together these represent about 80% of government receipts (1980), the remainder being divided fairly evenly between borrowing and items **2**, **3** and **4** above. In this section, we are concerned primarily with central government taxes.

Purposes The primary function of taxation is to raise revenue to finance government expenditure, but it may also be used to influence expenditure patterns, to redistribute income and wealth, and to reflect other social and political priorities.

Criteria for evaluation The relative merits of certain taxes are normally judged according to the following principles:

1. Fairness This is usually interpreted with regard to the ability of people to pay the tax. A **progressive tax** is one which takes a greater *proportion* of people's income as income rises, whilst a **regressive tax** accounts for a smaller *proportion* of high incomes than low incomes.

2. Effect on efficiency Within the economy as a whole, this refers to the effect of taxes on the allocation of resources. For example, does the tax discourage effort or enterprise, or compensate for the existence of externalities?

3. Administration This involves the cost of collecting taxes relative to the revenue raised and the convenience of complying with tax requirements (e.g. the amount of paperwork involved in various tax returns). This might be extended to a consideration of the *complexity* of tax legislation and the certainty of liability. Finally, it might include the ease with which non-payment can be avoided.

Direct taxes are those applied to the income of individuals and companies and to transfers of income and wealth. The two main items are income tax and corporation tax.

Income tax (40.9% of total taxation, U.K. 1979–80.) All individuals receive a personal allowance (dependent on marital status and certain allowable expenses, such as interest payments on mortgages) which is not subject to income tax. The remaining taxable income is taxed in progressively higher 'bands'. For example, in 1980 the first £11 250 of taxable income was subject to a tax of 30% (the 'basic rate'), rising in stages to a maximum marginal rate of 60% on taxable incomes in excess of £27 750. Only a very small proportion of income earners pay tax above the basic rate. Thus, although the marginal rate of tax is constant for most people (at 30%), the average rate of tax will rise with increased income as the personal allowance becomes a smaller proportion of gross income. In this sense, income tax can be classified as progressive.

The poverty trap However, income tax cannot be considered in isolation from other aspects of the tax system. The combination of income tax, a fixed percentage rate for national insurance contributions (on *all* earned income) and the loss of earnings-related benefits as income rises, can mean that an extra £1 of earned income *decreases* a person's disposable income. This represents an effective marginal tax rate of over 100%, affecting low income earners. It is an obvious defect in the income tax system, both in terms of 'fairness' and the incentive effect, known as the 'poverty trap'. Although applying to a relatively small number of people, it would clearly discourage overtime work, increase the attraction of activity in the black economy and (when taken in conjunction with forgone leisure and travel costs) may discourage some from working at all.

Fiscal drag If personal allowances and tax thresholds (at which higher marginal rates come into operation) are not increased in line with inflation, income tax payments will tend to rise in real terms. In his 1981 budget, for example, the Chancellor left personal allowances unchanged despite a double digit inflation rate. Administratively, this is a cheap alternative to raising the basic rate (with the political advantage of being less obvious to the average tax payer).

Advantages For the majority of tax payers, income tax has no apparent disincentive effects and, by its nature, is related to the ability to pay and is normally progressive in its effect.

Corporation tax (9.1% of total taxation, U.K. 1979–80) This is a tax on the profits of companies, whether distributed or retained. There is a threshold level combined with lower marginal rates for small firms (to compensate for their difficulties in raising external finance). The intricacies of the imputation system and the question of depreciation allowances are considered in the 'Finance' title in this series.

Indirect taxes are those applied to expenditure and the value-added to production.

Unit taxes are taxes of a fixed amount per unit of the good, regardless of its cost or price. If such taxes are not increased in line with inflation, their yield in real terms tends to decline. Thus, they may need to be adjusted at regular intervals in periods of high inflation.

Unit taxes (such as those on alcohol or tobacco, which accounted for 10.0% of total taxation, U.K. 1979–80) may be applied to goods with a relatively low responsiveness of the quantity demanded to changes in price, in order to increase government revenue, or to internalize the social costs which their consumption causes. Alternatively, they may be used to encourage more efficient consumption of resources such as petrol.

Value-added taxes (15.9% of total taxation, U.K. 1979–80) vary in direct proportion to the price of the good (or its cost of production). The current standard rate is 15%, but some products are exempted or zero-rated (in which case VAT embodied in inputs may be reclaimed). From the firm's viewpoint, the introduction of VAT imposed a considerable clerical burden, although this reduces the cost to the government of collecting and administering the tax.

Whilst the microeconomic effects of indirect taxes are considered in Chapter 6, it is apparent that increases in indirect taxes will increase the price level. If this increase in the cost of living is reflected in wage settlements, indirect taxes may contribute to an **inflationary spiral** caused by rising costs. On the other hand, an increase in indirect taxes will, of itself, only cause a once-and-for-all change in the retail price index, which will not contribute to a continuing process of inflation. Moreover, increased leakages from the circular flow (by means of increased indirect taxes) will have a deflationary effect on the level of aggregate demand, reducing an inflationary gap caused by excess demand.

Indirect taxes are sometimes said to be **regressive**. If low income groups spend a higher proportion of their income than high income groups, their indirect tax payments are likely to represent a higher proportion of their income. On the other hand, high income groups may spend a larger proportion of their income on goods which are subject to higher levels of indirect taxation.

Advantages The main advantages, for the state, of indirect taxes are the low costs of administration, the difficulty of evasion, and the fact that they do not have any disincentive effects. Also, they enable discrimination between different goods and services, and are relatively flexible.

Taxation and demand management
The most significant advantages of changes in taxation as opposed to changes in public expenditure as an instrument of fiscal policy are:

1. Reversibility Although changes in tax rates have administrative costs, policy can be much more readily reversed by using changes in taxation.

2. Immediacy Depending on the tax changes selected, the effect on aggregate demand is likely to be felt much more quickly.

3. Provision of services Changes in taxation do not (in themselves) affect the provision of services by government bodies, which might otherwise cause conflict with social and political objectives.

Budgetary policy
The annual budget is the occasion on which the Chancellor outlines his fiscal policy for the financial year. Because of the government's ability to borrow, its expenditure may exceed its revenue. This is termed 'deficit spending' and is traditionally associated with situations in which the government seeks to boost aggregate demand to take up spare capacity in the economy. Thus, in a budget deficit, the Chancellor would increase spending by a greater amount than taxes, for example. The financing of this deficit is considered below.

A **balanced budget** is one where government spending (G) and taxation (T) change by the same amount. If T decreases by £1bn, disposable income rises by the same amount, but some of this is saved or spent on imports, so that aggregate demand will rise by less than £1bn. On the other hand, a decrease in G of £1bn does decrease aggregate demand directly by £1bn, so that the net effect is contractionary. Conversely, if both G and T rise by the same amount, the net effect is likely to be expansionary. Thus, balanced budgets must be distinguished from *neutral budgets,* where the level of aggregate demand is left unaltered.

Deficit financing
The conventional Keynesian response to under-full

employment is to run a budget deficit, which is financed by
borrowing. During the 1970s a growing concern about the
effects of persistent deficit financing blossomed into government acceptance of an alternative economic doctrine,
known as *monetarism*. The main monetarist criticisms of
Keynesian demand management techniques are summarized (with considerable simplification) below.

1. Big Brother At the heart of the debate is a fundamental
difference of opinion about the proper role of the state in
economics. Monetarists favour free enterprise and competition, arguing that deficit financing has been used to increase
state influence in the economy, hampering competition and
discouraging private enterprise while perpetuating inefficient production in declining industries and holding back the
development of growth industries. This is often connected
with the disincentive effects of the increased taxation
necessary to support state economic activity.

2. Destabilization Monetarists argue that fiscal policy has
had the long-term effect of destabilizing the economy, causing cyclical fluctuations to become exaggerated. The main
reason for this, they argue, is that governments have
attempted to maintain demand at too high a level, discouraging factor mobility and building up inflationary
expectations, which are fed by the additional money
pumped into the economy by the government's profligacy.

3. Crowding out Interest rates are the price of borrowing
money. If government borrowing increases (to finance
budget deficits), interest rates will inevitably be forced up.
The government can afford to pay the higher interest rates
(by increasing taxes or simply borrowing to repay debt), but
private sector business is adversely affected:

(a) Higher interest rates increase the cost of holding
stocks. Perversely, this may cause firms to borrow more
(increasing the pressure on interest rates), and encour-
ages firms to cut current production to run down their
stocks. This will cause increased unemployment (which is
where the story started!).
(b) Higher interest rates make investment more costly,
and may therefore discourage increased efficiency and
innovation.
(c) Increased interest rates relative to those abroad tend to
increase the inflow of foreign currencies ('hot money'),
which has the effect of increasing the exchange rate. Higher
interest rates cause the price of U.K. exports in foreign
markets to rise relative to domestic prices, so that demand
falls. Firms which export a large proportion of their output
will face decreased profits and are therefore likely to reduce
their labour force, further increasing the depression.

4. The money supply The public sector borrowing
requirement (PSBR) includes the deficits of central and
local government and the public corporations. Whilst
including other factors, the budget deficit is an important

element in the PSBR. The government can borrow to finance the PSBR from three sources:

(a) *The non-bank private sector (NBPS)* This can take the form of non-marketable debt (such as savings certificates and premium bonds) or marketable debt ('government securities'). In either case, money will be taken from banks and paid to the government, tending to reduce the amount of money in circulation. Only if the NBPS holds additional notes and coins (which is a form of interest-free loan to the government) will the money supply be increased; this is a negligible amount.

(b) *The overseas sector* Similarly, borrowing from non-residents does not tend to increase the money supply.

(c) *The banking sector* If the government is forced to borrow from the banking community in the form of treasury bills (short-term debt), the credit base of the banks expands enabling them to create new deposits, which directly increases the money supply.

The monetarist argument is that persistent increases in the PSBR have forced the government into greater borrowing from the banking sector, causing the money supply to increase much faster than the output of goods and services. Too much money chasing too few goods causes inflation, with consequent decreased competitiveness and increased unemployment.

Consequently, monetarists argue that the role of government in stabilizing the economy should be limited to the task of creating a stable environment in which enterprise can flourish. This is best achieved, they say, by reducing the intervention of government, balancing government expenditure and revenue, and controlling the money supply in order to remove inflationary pressures.

The neo-Keynesians accept that control of the money supply is a necessary (but not sufficient) factor in reducing inflation, but argue that this is not incompatible with deficit financing: this is simply a matter of neutralizing the monetary effects of an increase in the PSBR. They point to the disadvantages of the price mechanism as a means of resource allocation (see Chapter 1) and to the enormous cost in terms of increased unemployment and liquidated firms which monetarist policies would involve in the cause of removing inflation. It is likely, they say, that the cure would be worse than the disease, and that inflation can be controlled by fiscal and direct means, provided that the effects on the money supply are taken into account. In the next chapter, we consider the problems of inflation and unemployment more fully.

Chapter 4

Inflation and Unemployment

Definition Inflation is the process of a persistent and generalized increase in the level of prices in an economy.

Measurement Inflation is normally measured as a percentage increase on the previous year's price level (as indicated by the Retail Price Index). The Retail Price Index (RPI) measures the cost of purchasing a representative 'basket' of goods and services, intended to be typical of the average household's expenditure. Each of the items – which range from food and drink to housing and consumer durables – is weighted according to the proportion of household expenditure for which it accounts, which in turn is determined from the government's extensive Family Expenditure Survey.

The Index is related to a base date, at which its value is taken as 100. Thus, if the RPI stood at 110 one year from the base date, this would represent a 10% increase in the price level. This does not mean that each item in the 'basket' has risen in price by 10%, but that the overall cost of the representative selection of goods has risen by this amount. Nor does it mean that people are 10% worse off than a year before, since the RPI does not account for changes in income or direct taxes.

Inflation and economic policy

The control of inflation has been considered a prime objective of the government's economic policy in recent years for a variety of reasons (the relative significance of each depending on the economic and political beliefs of individual governments).

1. Inflation is unfair This argument relates to the belief that those worst affected by inflation are those least able to look after themselves, in particular people (such as pensioners and the unemployed) whose incomes are fixed in money terms or who are in weak bargaining positions. Clearly, inflation will decrease the purchasing power of fixed money incomes over time, and others may find their money incomes increasing less quickly than the price level.

2. International competitiveness If the inflation rate in the U.K. is higher than in other countries, exports from the U.K. will suffer decreased price competitiveness in foreign markets, whilst other countries' imports into the U.K. will gain a relative price advantage. Other things being equal, this will tend to reduce the sterling exchange rate. Although this may restore price competitiveness, the cost of imports into the U.K. rises, which in turn will add to the rate of increase of the domestic price level.

3. Savings and interest rates Savers will suffer as a result of inflation if interest rates are lower than the annual rate of price increases. On the other hand, if interest rates rise in line with relatively high inflation rates, inflows of savings from abroad will prevent the exchange rate from falling to restore the competitiveness of U.K. exports.

4. Investment and employment If inflation rates are high or (perhaps even more important) unstable, the investment decision-making process may be adversely affected. With a high inflation rate, the *gross* return on capital will need to be relatively high to guarantee a positive *real* return on an investment project which would justify the opportunity cost of the funds involved. Thus, investment projects, which would be perfectly viable with low and stable rates of inflation, may have to be ruled out when there is uncertainty about future levels of inflation.

Moreover, high levels of inflation may cause firms to have a pessimistic view of future revenue flows from an investment project. This may be justified by expectations of government measures designed to decrease demand to reduce inflationary pressure, or by the experience of decreased foreign demand due to reduced price competitiveness of exports. Clearly, a reduction in investment expenditure will (via the multiplier effect) reduce the level of employment. Insofar as inflationary pressures are transmitted via rises in unit wage costs, the investment which does occur may be specifically aimed at substituting capital for labour.

5. Expectations It has been shown that relatively high rates of inflation adversely affect business expectations, so that investment and employment tend to decline. Additionally, consumers' expectations will affect their current actions. In the labour market, for example, people will build into their wage demands a sum intended to counter-balance the expected change in the cost of living. Assuming no corresponding increase in productivity, this will raise unit wage costs, contributing to further price increases: an example of the self-fulfilling prophecy. The decline in price competitiveness will obviously adversely affect employment, investment and economic growth.

6. Standard of living If inflation tends to have the effects described above, then it is inevitable that the economy will operate with spare capacity, i.e. below optimum efficiency. The economy will grow less quickly than would be possible, which means that the average standard of living will also be less than would otherwise be possible.

The U.K. experience
In the previous chapter, inflation was associated with a situation in which aggregate monetary demand at the full employment level of output exceeded the economy's physical capacity to produce. In such a case, zero inflation could be coincidental with full employment. This obviously does not agree with observations of inflation and unemployment in the U.K. in recent years.

The Keynesian model presented in Chapter 2 can be adapted to allow for the co-existence of inflation and unemployment by introducing differences in the demand for different industrial sectors. Some sectors will experience bottlenecks in the supply of factors long before the economy as a whole could be said to be at full employment, whilst others, in long-term decline, may have spare capacity even during the boom period of the business cycle. Thus, unit costs may start to rise in some sectors (where there is excess demand) below the full employment level of output. As aggregate demand increases, so more industries experience such bottlenecks and the rate of inflation rises as the level of unemployment falls.

Thus, it is possible to develop the idea of a trade-off between inflation and unemployment as a policy objective: the lower the level of unemployment, the higher the rate of inflation. This has been supported by empirical studies on the U.K. economy between 1861 and 1957. However, during the 1970s this relationship has been questioned, since a tendency was observed for both inflation and unemployment to rise. It has been argued that this reflects the effects of expectations of future inflation being built into wage demands. This causes a higher level of inflation to be associated with any given level of unemployment, and leads to the monetarist view that increased levels of unemployment are a necessary but unfortunate short-term measure to reduce inflationary expectations and to restore the traditional trade-off.

COUNTER-INFLATIONARY POLICY

The policy which is appropriate to remove inflation depends entirely on the analysis of the cause of inflation. There are many conflicting views on the causes of inflation, and the discussion here is limited to just a few of the mainstream arguments in the context of relatively high levels of unemployment.

Monetarism

In the previous chapter, it was explained that monetarists argue that if the money supply grows faster than the economy's output, individuals and firms will find themselves with larger money balances than they desire to hold. They spend the 'surplus', but since the supply of goods and services has not risen proportionately, this creates excess demand causing general increases in the price level. Moreover, we have seen that inflationary expectations result in higher levels of inflation being associated with rising unemployment. Thus, unemployment can only be reduced in the long term if inflationary expectations are removed, and this may require higher levels of unemployment in the short term.

There are two basic inter-linked elements in a typical monetarist strategy:

1. Reducing the rate of growth of the money supply.
2. Decreasing inflationary expectations.

These may involve a variety of specific measures:

(a) Reducing the PSBR This facilitates the control of the money supply and prevents 'artificial' reductions in unemployment below the natural rate. The long-term objective would be a balanced budget.

(b) Monetary controls In line with their free market philosophy, monetarists usually reject direct controls on bank lending (the main means by which the money supply is increased). Instead, they prefer to let interest rates – the price of money – do the job. As a major borrower, the government (by bidding higher prices for the savings of the non-bank private sector) can have a significant effect on interest rates. By this means, it can deprive the banking system of part of the funds on which their lending ability depends, as well as decreasing the demand for loans (by raising the cost of borrowing).

(c) Increased competitiveness The combined effect of decreased aggregate demand and higher interest rates will require firms in the private sector to increase efficiency if they are to survive. Over-manning will be reduced, and lower wage settlements and fewer industrial disputes should result, as union bargaining power is reduced by the existence of higher unemployment and the threat of company closures.

Reduction of the PSBR may also have the effect of increasing competitiveness in the public sector: indeed, it may in part be achieved by selling some of the commercially viable parts of state industries to the private sector ('privatization'). But if the PSBR is reduced by removing subsidies to state industries and restricting their borrowing ability, the consequent price rises would initially contribute to the existing inflationary spiral.

(d) Psychological measures Since expectations play an important role in perpetuating inflation, measures aimed at boosting confidence in the government's strategy are of obvious importance. The announcement of medium-term targets for the growth of the money supply and the PSBR, cash limits on public sector expenditure, and wage 'norms' for public sector employees is designed to demonstrate a firm commitment to reducing inflation and thereby to changing expectations. This may be propagated by careful explanation of policies, and exhortation and propaganda to subvert the credibility of alternative strategies. The more people believe that the government will take the measures necessary to control inflation, the greater the likelihood of the policy's success.

Criticisms of monetarism

The monetarist philosophy may be contested on two main grounds: its theoretical basis, and its factual effects and effectiveness.

Theoretical arguments These are really quite technical, but the following is a summary, in simple terms, of the main areas of dispute.

1. Causality Just because inflation tends to follow increases in the money supply, this does not necessarily mean that the increase in the money supply causes the inflation. After all, the sale of cup final tickets precedes the cup final, but no-one would argue that it is the sale of tickets which causes the cup final to take place. In this example, the anticipation of the subsequent event (the cup final) has caused the prior event (the sale of tickets). It might be argued that the relationship between inflation and the money supply has at least an element of this reverse causality.

Critics of monetarism often look to the direct causes of cost increases: the cost of raw materials, wage rates and interest rates, for example. Monetarists would say that these are simply the means by which the excess money supply is converted into its inevitable inflationary consequences. We consider 'cost-push' theories in more detail below.

2. The transmission mechanism Neo-Keynesians argue that the primary effect of increases in the money supply is felt in the markets for financial assets, and hence is reflected in interest rates. If the excess money supply is not totally absorbed in this way, it may feed through into the markets for physical assets and hence have inflationary consequences. Neo-Keynesians believe, however, that this is a much less direct effect than the monetarists say. Thus, they argue that fiscal policy offers a more direct means of economic control than monetary policy.

3. The velocity of circulation This argument refers to the stability and predictability of the relationship between an increase in the money supply and the consequent effect on prices. If the frequency with which each unit of the money supply changes hands during a given time period is subject to wild fluctuation, then the usefulness of monetary policy is again open to question when related to counter-inflationary policy.

Pragmatic criticisms Even ignoring these significant objections on theoretical grounds, monetarism has been criticized in terms of the effects it has on an economy and on the practicality of implementing the measures necessary to work the monetarist miracle, particularly in the context of an economy already operating with considerable spare capacity. The following is a summary of the main criticisms of the Thatcher government's attempts to effect a monetarist solution to the U.K.'s economic problems in the period following its election in 1979.

1. Monetary control There are several problems involved in what might appear to be a simple task: controlling the money supply.

(a) Firstly, it is necessary to decide which measure of the money supply is the appropriate target. In the U.K., there are at least five monetary measures which might be considered appropriate targets, but they are observed to change at different rates.

(b) A money supply measure which has demonstrated a strong statistical relationship with inflation could be selected, but once this is used as a policy target it may cease to exhibit this close statistical correlation, as measures to restrict its growth simply result in the money supply growing in ways which are only reflected in the other measures of the money supply. This phenomenon is referred to as Goodhart's Law. Control of the money supply is often compared to squeezing a balloon: squeeze one part of the balloon successfully and the other parts of the balloon only increase in size instead.

(c) Even when a suitable money supply target (or range of targets) is selected, the institutional controls do not exist to achieve such a target, since the main source of increases in the money supply (bank deposits) are determined by the decisions of non-governmental bodies. Even when new controls on the creation of bank deposits have been implemented, the financial system has shown a remarkable capacity to find ways around the spirit of such controls.

(d) When a government avows such complete faith in monetarism, failure to achieve its monetary targets must inevitably have an adverse effect on inflationary expectations.

2. Effects on business Monetarists expect strict control of the money supply to encourage increased efficiency and to leave firms leaner and fitter to take advantage of the available opportunities in the post-inflationary recovery. Unfortunately, several factors may negate these hopes.

(a) Decreased demand causes profits to fall and stocks to rise. Despite higher interest rates, firms may be forced to borrow more to finance the increased cost of holding stocks. As firms attempt to run down their stocks they must meet the cost of making employees redundant, and may find that unit costs rise given a smaller scale of production. These factors tend to reinforce cost-push pressures towards higher prices.

(b) Exporters are likely to be hit even harder since higher interest rates are likely to attract foreign currency, causing the exchange rates to rise. As discussed in the next chapter, given certain assumptions, this will tend to make our exports less competitive in foreign markets, whilst domestic producers suffer as imported substitutes gain a price advantage from the exchange rate.

(c) The monetarist squeeze is indiscriminate in its effects. Often, it is the progressive, high growth firm which is committed to a programme of massive investment, and which has made a substantial international marketing effort, that is most vulnerable to increased interest rates and exchange rates. Inefficient and declining firms may go to the wall as predicted, but they may take with them many efficient and expanding companies which would have otherwise been expected to thrive.

3. Conflicting objectives It has been argued by the critics of monetarism that the effects of a monetarist strategy may be worse than the consequences of the inflation that it seeks to remove.

(a) The short-term increase in unemployment, which a monetarist strategy involves, has undesirable economic, social and political effects (see page 60).

(b) Increased unemployment imposes increased statutory public expenditure and decreases receipts from personal and corporate taxation, thus tending to increase the PSBR and make control of the money supply more difficult.

(c) Reductions in public expenditure (in an attempt to decrease the PSBR) are likely either to further decrease demand or to reduce the services provided for those least able to look after themselves: a conflict with the social objectives which the reduction of inflation is intended to achieve.

(d) The objectives of monetarism are long term, but the adverse short-term consequences may, in a democracy, lead to a change of government and economic strategy such that any long-term benefits which might exist are never gained.

(e) We have seen that high interest rates and exchange rates tend to decrease domestic demand and economic growth. In such an environment the increased investment which is necessary to raise productivity and competitiveness is unlikely to be forthcoming, so that the duration of the recession is prolonged.

Alternative strategies

Monetarist economists are convinced that there is no alternative to the bitter pill of the strategy which has been described. As has been shown above, they have been particularly concerned to point to the detrimental effects of deficit spending as a means of combating economic depression. The critics of monetarist strategy seek ways of reducing inflation without increasing unemployment.

Cost-push inflation It can be argued that inflation may be initiated by an *autonomous* increase in the costs of production rather than by excess monetary demand. If this were the case, measures directed to controlling such cost increases would be appropriate to the removal of inflation. The significance of any individual increase in costs will depend on the proportion of total costs for which the given factor accounts. Since the cost of imported materials is generally considered outside the control of domestic economic policy, most attention has focused on the control of labour costs, which are the major component of total costs for most firms.

An autonomous increase in labour costs is most likely to

occur during the upswing of the business cycle. It may originate in expanding sectors, where firms are able either to absorb increased labour costs through increased productivity or are able to pass on the increased costs in the form of higher prices without a proportionate contraction of demand. However, if other groups of workers successfully imitate this increase in real wages through relativities bargaining in sectors where the increased costs cannot be absorbed, there will be a general rise in prices which will undermine the initial increase in real wages. In the next wage round, workers seek to restore the original increase in real wages through further pay demands based on their inflationary expectations, and so the wage–price spiral continues. Inevitably, unemployment will start to rise as exports become less competitive and imported goods gain a greater share of domestic markets.

Such a wage–price spiral cannot perpetuate itself in the absence of a complementary increase in the money supply, but we have already observed some of the difficulties involved in using monetary policy to counteract the spiral. Hence, some commentators see incomes policy as a means of reducing inflationary pressures without increasing unemployment.

Incomes policies

There are many forms of incomes policies, ranging from the informal agreement to legislative measures. Normally, an incomes policy results from consultation between government, management and trade unions, and is applied to the wages or earnings of all employees. Other factor incomes, such as profits and interest, may be controlled by discretionary taxation. The main problems which such policies tend to encounter include:

1. Trade union opposition Unions see collective bargaining, in which they represent the interests of their members, as an important function, and are generally unwilling to concede to the constraints of an incomes policy except under crisis circumstances, and only then for a limited time period. In the U.K. during the 1970s, under both Labour and Conservative governments, union opposition to incomes policy has resulted in major industrial disruption and has contributed to the electoral defeat of the government.

2. Loopholes It is very difficult to monitor incomes policies sufficiently closely to ensure that their restrictions are adhered to. Even where the word of an agreement is enforced, its spirit may be infringed by bogus promotions and job re-classifications, increased non-monetary benefits and so forth. Some groups – such as the self-employed and those employed on a commission basis – are virtually impossible to control.

If an incomes policy permits 'special cases' and productivity deals, these may be widely abused; if it does not, the policy tends to be inflexible, unfair to certain groups of workers, and reduces incentives to increased effort.

3. Resource allocation Since differences in incomes tend to re-allocate resources between different uses, the imposition of an incomes policy may prevent efficient resource re-allocation, leading to labour shortages in certain occupations. If the incomes policy permits flat-rate increases, differentials (expressed in percentage terms) will be distorted, and may give rise to skill shortages as the incentive to undertake increased training and responsibility is reduced.

4. Inflationary backlash In the U.K., incomes policies have always been introduced as a reaction to a specific crisis and as a temporary measure. The longer the policy lasts, the more difficult it has been to achieve its continued acceptance, and as the policy is relaxed there is a tendency for suppressed income increases to flood the labour market in an inflationary backlash which can easily negate the achievements of the period of restraint.

This is by no means a comprehensive list of the problems which are associated with incomes policies. It is difficult to assess their success, since it would be necessary to compare the actual outcome with what would have otherwise occurred and, even then, the effect of an inflationary backlash when the policy is removed must be taken into account.

Price controls
In the short term, it is clearly possible to manipulate the Retail Price Index to give the impression of a downward trend in inflationary pressures by such measures as:

1. Reducing the rate of VAT.
2. Increasing subsidies to private companies.
3. Holding down the prices of nationalized industries' goods and services.
4. Statutory controls on the prices which firms may charge for their products.

Advantages Given that the RPI is a major point of reference in formulating wage demands, these measures would tend to depress wage settlements. Statutory controls would incline firms to be more resilient in the face of wage demands in order to protect their profitability. Increased price competitiveness would boost employment in export and import substitute industries.

If expectations are a major factor in the perpetuation of an inflationary spiral, these controls would actually help to remove one of the underlying causes of inflation and, insofar as they result in restricting wage pressures, they would assist in reducing cost-push pressures.

Disadvantages The combined effect of measures **1., 2., 3.** and **4.** above would be to increase the PSBR (other things being equal). This might be overcome either by increasing rates of direct taxation (which would be likely to undermine the claimed advantages of the measures), or as a result of increased tax revenue, resulting from higher levels of economic activity (since the measures increase aggregate demand), coupled with decreased payments of unemployment and welfare benefits. However, if increased government borrowing did result, with consequent pressure on the money supply, the rate of increase of monetary demand might exceed the rate at which output expands, exacerbating inflationary pressures.

Statutory controls on prices tend to decrease profitability over time, which is likely to discourage investment and result in decreased price competitiveness in the long term. If supply does not respond proportionately to increased demand, shortages occur which may result in increased import penetration, surreptitious price increases, black markets and so forth. Moreover, increased resilience of firms to wage demands may result in increased industrial disputes, causing decreased output and profitability.

Productivity

If the underlying problem is lack of price competitiveness and monetary demand outstripping domestic production, one positive means of improving the situation is to improve productivity. As we have seen, this is the long-term aim of a monetarist strategy (to be achieved through the price mechanism), but others argue that increased productivity can be fostered directly through government intervention. The alleged advantages of such a scheme would be that it tackles the problem of inflation at its roots, is effected more quickly than a monetarist strategy, and reduces unemployment at the same time.

The possible measures which might be introduced to this end include the following:

1. Direct investment in improved productive capacity in nationalized industries.
2. Improved incentives for fixed investment in private industries, e.g. increased grants.
3. Government finance for risk ventures in the 'sun-rise industries', e.g. micro-electronics and robotics.

Monetarists would, of course, dismiss this as 'spending our way out of recession', and would point to the implications for the PSBR and the money supply. However, such a scheme is *qualitatively* different from the methods which Keynesian governments have used, essentially as short-term tactics for reducing unemployment, e.g. public works schemes and support for ailing public sector enterprises such as shipbuilding and steel. It adds to output and efficiency as it boosts demand through the multiplier effects which would result. It is likely that increased supply would lag behind the increase in demand, so that the initial monetary effects may need to be neutralized.

Unemployment

Inflation and unemployment have been considered as twin evils in our discussion of slumpflation. In the final section of this chapter, we look specifically at the policy problems related to the high levels of unemployment experienced in recent years.

Labour is a scarce resource with a finite productive life, whether it is used or not. The time a person spends in the dole queue is never regained. From the point of view of productive potential, therefore, unemployment represents an opportunity cost expressed in terms of forgone output of goods and services. There are more tangible financial costs of unemployment in a modern welfare state: increased government expenditure on benefits, redundancy payments, reduced tax revenue and so forth.

Perhaps even more significant are the social effects of prolonged periods of involuntary unemployment. Work, for most people, provides not simply a means of income to provide for the individual and his or her dependents, but a sense of identity, purpose and usefulness. Unemployment may involve financial hardship (particularly where the individual is committed to regular payments such as mortgages, loans and credit agreements), but also brings with it social and psychological effects of an immeasurable magnitude. Where young people are involved, particularly, the boredom and frustration may find expression in acts of violence and vandalism which take their financial toll. The longer term economic, social and political effects of such disenchantment remain to be seen.

Measurement The unemployment rate is the percentage of the total labour force who register at government employment offices as able and willing to work but who are not in current employment. There are many reasons why official statistics may to some extent be misleading:

1. Young people who would prefer employment may remain in full-time education after the age of 16 or take government-sponsored training or work experience schemes, simply because they are unable to secure jobs and have no prospect of doing so.

2. Some women, who would not be eligible for benefits, may choose not to register as unemployed (despite wanting and actively seeking for jobs) if recorded vacancies are low.

3. Some older people may take premature retirement if the prospects of finding alternative employment are limited.

These factors indicate an element of under-statement in the official statistics. On the other hand, there may be elements of over-statement:

1. People who register as unemployed but who are in fact employed (cf. the hidden economy, pages 26–28).

2. The registered unemployed who have no intention of taking a job if offered one.

3. Those genuinely seeking employment who are extremely unlikely (e.g. through physical or mental disability) to secure offers.

Causes of unemployment It is misleading to consider unemployment as a single problem. Unemployment results from a number of factors, which need to be separately identified if appropriate remedies are to be found.

1. Voluntary unemployment We have seen above that there are reasons why people may choose to remain unemployed. For some others, unemployment may be a rational decision: the combined effects of tax liability, loss of earnings-related benefits and costs associated with employment (such as travel expenses) may make low paid employment financially less attractive than unemployment.

2. Frictional unemployment At any one time, some people will be temporarily unemployed whilst moving from one job to another. Having chosen to leave one job (and possibly having already secured a new position), people often take a short break: particularly if their move involves a sacrifice of holiday entitlement. This form of frictional unemployment represents the largest group of those who are voluntarily unemployed. A high degree of industrial and occupational mobility of labour (indicated by high levels of frictional unemployment) are usually considered indicative of a healthy and dynamic economy.

These two forms of voluntary unemployment are of minor significance both quantitatively and in terms of their economic significance. Attempts to reduce their level by boosting aggregate demand are unlikely to be successful and would almost certainly have inflationary consequences. Some marginal reduction might be achieved by varying the benefit regulations, but from the policy viewpoint it is the different major forms of involuntary unemployment which need closest attention:

3. Cyclical unemployment This is unemployment which results from deficient aggregate demand during a recession. In the short term, at least, this can be remedied by deficit spending, but we have seen that there is some controversy over the long-term effects of such strategies.

4. Regional unemployment During the nineteenth century certain industries became heavily concentrated in particular geographical regions, e.g. steel production in South Wales and shipbuilding in the North-East. As foreign production increased, these industries suffered from increased competition at home and abroad. As the structure of world demand and production changes over time, and as new industries emerge, so the long-term decline of these regionally concentrated industries has had a particularly severe local effect, causing marked inequalities in unemployment rates between regions, as labour tends to be geographically immobile.

Generally, U.K. policy has been concerned to 'take work to the workers' in these regions rather than to encourage geographical mobility. This is justified to prevent problems of over-crowding, strain on social capital, congestion and so forth in the growth areas, whilst avoiding the under-utilization of such resources in the depressed regions. Thus, the policy has centred around attracting new or expanding firms to locate in the depressed areas, using incentives such as advance-built factories, short-term exemption from local taxation, reduced rents, investment grants, etc.

The effectiveness of such policy is difficult to measure, since it is necessary to attempt comparison with what might have happened in the absence of regional policy. If, in the absence of the incentives, firms would have had lower costs in other regions, the policy may have the effect of increasing real production costs. If the regional incentives (paid from general taxation) result in higher profits for shareholders, then a regressive redistribution of income may be involved. Moreover, regional policy may be used to postpone the decline of 'lame-duck' industries and may thereby hamper the efficient re-allocation of resources.

Finally, a competitive element may arise between regions or between countries to attract, for example, the new investment of multinationals. There have been alleged instances of multinationals receiving regional aid but failing to create the promised employment opportunities, or changing location once optimum use of the regional benefits has been enjoyed, or (having reaped the benefits) threatening closure in an attempt to secure further government aid.

5. Technological unemployment Unemployment resulting from the obsolescence of products or labour skills is often closely linked to regional unemployment. Perhaps the most challenging policy problem for the rest of this century will be to cope with the new skill requirements of the micro-electronic age and the redeployment of those manual and semi-skilled workers whose functions are taken over by computers and robots.

In the past, fears of mass unemployment resulting from major technological innovations in the production process have proved unfounded. It is not unnatural, however, that the staggering potential of laser technology, micro-biology, robotics and micro-electronics (the 'sun-rise industries'), and the gathering cumulative pace of technological change, should again foster such fears, particularly since their introduction has coincided with the deepest depression experienced during the post-1945 period. But, as with other major innovations, these industries will undoubtedly create new employment opportunities, increase productive potential in existing industries and open up new markets.

Chapter 5

International Trade

Why do countries trade? The obvious answer is because they benefit: consumers have a wider range of choice, firms have access to larger markets, a fuller use of a country's resources may be facilitated, and the country's growth rate may be augmented by the stimulus of increased injections into the circular flow of income (in the form of exports).

Theoretical basis

Such advantages are obvious where different countries have an absolute advantage in the production of a good: the resource cost of the U.K. trying to produce its own coffee, for example, would be enormous relative to Brazil. So it is obviously more efficient for the U.K. to use its resources to produce, say, synthetic fibres, which it could trade with Brazil for coffee. In this case, specialization and trade clearly have the potential to benefit both countries.

Comparative advantage

Not so obvious is the situation in which one country may be better than another in the production of all commodities, and yet where trade can still be demonstrated to be mutually beneficial. This proposition is explained by the principle of comparative advantage, which can be demonstrated by a simple example.

For ease of explanation, we use a two product, two country model, in which we assume no transport costs, perfect factor mobility between the production of two goods, and constant average costs as output is increased. The table below shows the output per period of two goods, A and B, for a given identical input of resources in the two countries, X and Y.

	COUNTRY X	COUNTRY Y
GOOD A	50 units	10 units
GOOD B	10 units	5 units

Country X is more efficient in converting the input of resources into output of both of the two goods. However, if we convert these figures into domestic opportunity costs (e.g. what quantity of good A must be forgone in order to produce an additional unit of good B), we can begin to appreciate the basis of the possibility for specialization and trade.

Domestic opportunity cost of producing one unit of:	COUNTRY X	COUNTRY Y
GOOD A	0.2 B	0.5 B
GOOD B	5.0 A	2.0 A

Whilst country X has an *absolute advantage* in the production of both goods, on the basis of the comparison of opportunity costs it has a *comparative disadvantage* in the production of good B: it has to forgo a greater quantity of good A in order to produce an additional unit of good B than country Y does.

In the absence of trade, if each country applied one unit of resources to the production of each good, total production would be 60 units of A and 15 units of B. However, increased total production is possible if the countries specialize according to the principle of comparative advantage. For example, if Y uses both its resource units to produce good B, and X uses 1.5 units to produce good A and only half of a resource unit to produce good B, total production would increase by 15 units of good A, as shown below:

	COUNTRY X	COUNTRY Y	TOTAL
GOOD A	$1.5 \times 50 = 75$	0	75
GOOD B	$0.5 \times 10 = 5$	$2 \times 5 = 10$	15

Trade will be beneficial provided that country X demands less than half a unit of good B for each unit of good A exported, and that country Y demands less than 5 units of good A for each unit of good B it exports. Thus, the terms of trade would be better than the domestic opportunity cost of producing the traded goods. If terms of trade are agreed so that 1 unit of B is exchanged for 4 units of A, the new opportunity costs are as shown below.

Opportunity cost of one unit of each good:	COUNTRY X	COUNTRY Y
GOOD A	0.2 B	0.25 B (import)
GOOD B	4.0 A (import)	2.0 A

Whilst comparative advantage is useful in demonstrating the underlying rationale of international trade, we shall need to examine other advantages which may arise from trade and other explanations of the development of trade. Moreover, despite the inherent advantages of trade in terms of opportunity cost, there may be conflicting objectives which combine to encourage *protection* of a country's domestic industries. Before we can examine these aspects of international trade, it is necessary to understand the role of the balance of payments and exchange rates.

THE BALANCE OF PAYMENTS

Definition The balance of payments is the annual statement of transactions of a country's households, firms and public authorities (collectively termed 'residents') with the residents of other countries.

Table 7 shows the balances of the three constituent parts of the balance of payments: the current account, capital transactions and official financing. This tends to hide the

£ million

CURRENT ACCOUNT		
Visible balance		+ 1178
Invisibles:		
Services balance	+ 4188	
Interest, profits and dividends	− 38	
Transfers balance	− 2122	
Invisibles balance		+ 2028
CURRENT ACCOUNT BALANCE		+ 3206
Investment and other capital transactions		− 1475
Balancing item		− 539
BALANCE FOR OFFICIAL FINANCING		+ 1192
Allocation of SDRs		+ 180
		+ 1372
OFFICIAL FINANCING		
Net transactions with overseas monetary authorities		− 140
Foreign currency borrowing		− 941
Change in official reserves		− 291
		− 1372

Table 7. U.K. Summary Balance of Payments 1980 (Source: C.S.O. *United Kingdom Balance of Payments,* HMSO, 1981, Table 1.1)

magnitude of trade: in 1980, exports of U.K. goods were valued at roughly £47bn and invisible credits at about £25bn (relative to GNP of £193bn).

Balance of trade
The visible balance (or 'balance of trade') refers only to the difference between the export and import of *goods*. During the 1960s and '70s, the visible balance was in persistent deficit (apart from 1971), reaching crisis proportions between 1973 and 1976 following the oil price increases under the OPEC agreement and a boom in other commodity prices. During the 1980s, U.K. exports of oil are likely to improve the visible balance, but this may conceal weaknesses in other aspects of export performance.

The nature of the U.K.'s visible trade has changed substantially in the post-war era. It has moved from being an importer of food and raw materials and an exporter of manufactured products, trading mainly with the Commonwealth and other sterling area countries, to trading predominantly by an exchange of manufactured goods, increasingly with other European countries.

Invisibles balance
The table shows the three main components of invisible

trade: services; interest, profits and dividends; and transfers. Services include sea transport, civil aviation, travel and financial services (such as banking and insurance). When foreign residents buy such services from U.K. firms, there is an inflow of foreign currency indicated as a credit in the invisibles account. An inflow of currency can also result from assets owned in foreign countries which yield interest or profits. The main item under the 'transfers' heading is the government's contributions and subscriptions to international organizations (such as the EEC). It also includes government aid to developing countries and certain other public and private sector international currency transfers.

Throughout the post-war period, the U.K.'s invisible balance has been in surplus, and this has often offset deficits on visible trade. In terms of comparative advantage, it might be argued that there is a net exchange of U.K. services for imported goods.

Current account balance

The difference between the U.K.'s receipts of currency from foreigners for the provision of goods and services, and from transfers, and its residents' expenditure on foreign goods and services, and transfers to foreign residents, is known as the balance of payments on current account. It is this balance which indicates the ability of the country to 'pay its way' in current transactions with foreign countries, and it is changes in this balance which may prompt government remedial policy under certain circumstances.

Investment and other capital transactions

International currency flows can also result from the acquisition or sale of capital assets, and from transactions in financial assets.

In the short term, investment overseas represents a capital outflow, but future flows of revenue (in the form of interest, profits and dividends) would be shown as credits in the invisibles account. The converse argument applies to investment in this country by foreign residents.

Similarly, international transactions in financial assets affect the international currency flow. These include overseas currency borrowing and lending, purchases and sales of government securities, and credit instruments. Transactions in financial assets tend to be more volatile than other elements of the balance of payments, and are particularly influenced by differences in interest rates between countries and anticipated changes in exchange rates. The mobility of such funds has caused them to be dubbed 'hot money'.

Official financing

The sum of these balances shows the net currency flow during the year (although this is modified for statistical reasons by a 'balancing item', which represents the net total of errors and omissions arising throughout the accounts, resulting mainly from timing errors and changes in exchange rates). This 'balance for official financing' (plus certain occasional transactions involving the IMF) must be exactly matched by changes in the foreign reserves, or by increasing or reducing the country's foreign indebtedness.

If the net currency flow is positive (as in Table 7), debt may be repaid or the reserves increased, each of these being shown (by convention) as a negative sign in the 'official financing' account. The converse applies if the net currency flow is negative. Since official financing must, by definition, equal the net currency flow, it is sometimes said that 'the balance of payments always balances', but this is merely an accounting identity; government policy will be directed to the overall currency flow and particularly the current account balance.

Equilibrium in the balance of payments is said to occur where the desired net currency flow is achieved without the need for deliberate government policy measures aimed at influencing international trade (such as domestic deflation to decrease imports, monetary policy aimed at attracting capital inflows or import controls).

EXCHANGE RATES

Definition The exchange rate is the price of one country's currency denominated in terms of another country's currency.

From 1945 until the early 1970s, most western countries participated in a stable exchange rate scheme organized by the International Monetary Fund (IMF), known as the 'adjustable peg' system. Under this scheme, each country accepted responsibility for maintaining the price of its currency within given limits of its 'par value' except in the case of fundamental disequilibrium, when a devaluation or revaluation could be arranged. The main aims of this policy were to encourage trade through exchange rate stability and certainty, and to place a responsibility on governments to take the necessary corrective actions when their balance of payments accounts were in disequilibrium.

Floating exchange rates

Since the early 1970s, most countries have allowed their currencies to float, i.e. their exchange rates fluctuate on the foreign exchange market according to the pressures of demand and supply. Increased demand for a country's currency will tend to raise the exchange rate (other things being equal), whilst increased supply will tend to lower it. This is not to say that governments have no influence over their exchange rates; they may intervene directly to supply or demand their own country's currency in order to influence its price, or they may take actions which are directly intended to influence demand or supply.

The main advantage claimed for floating exchange rates is that they tend to correct disequilibrium in the balance of payments automatically. We can demonstrate the effects of changes in the exchange rate by means of an example.

If we consider the trade in two goods between two countries, ignoring differences in indirect taxes and transport costs, we can see the price changes resulting from a change in exchange rates. With an exchange rate of £1 = $2, the U.K. produces good A at a domestic price of £100 and the U.S.A. produces good B at a domestic price of $200. In this situation, the prices of the goods when traded (given our assumptions) would be identical.

If the sterling exchange rate falls ('depreciates') so that £1 = $1.75, the domestic prices of both goods are assumed to remain unchanged, but their prices in foreign markets will alter. In the U.K., the imported good B will now cost £116 (= $200 ÷ 1.75), whilst in the U.S.A. the imported good A will sell at $175 (= £100 × 1.75). That is to say, a depreciation of a country's currency raises the price of its imports relative to domestic products, other things being equal, and lowers the price of its exports relative to the prices of foreign producers. Thus, at first sight, it seems likely that imports will fall and exports will rise, which will tend to counteract the balance of payments disequilibrium. However, this depends on several other factors.

1. The price elasticity of demand (PED)
A good's PED is the responsiveness of the quantity demanded to a change in its price. If, for example, the PED for U.K. exports was measured as one, this would mean that, for a 1% fall in the U.K. export prices, demand would rise by 1% (and so total export expenditure would remain unchanged). A figure greater than one would indicate a more than proportionate rise in demand relative to the price change. (PED is considered in more detail in Chapter 6.)

Clearly if the same quantity of imports and exports is sold after a depreciation, the current balance will worsen. It can be shown that if the sum of a country's PED for imports and another countries' PED for its exports is greater than one, then the currency flow (on current account) will improve (the 'Marshall–Lerner condition').

2. The price elasticity of supply (PES)
PES measures the responsiveness of the quantity supplied to a change in its price. Even with favourable price elasticities of demand, the current balance will not improve unless and until U.K. producers (in our example) respond to the additional demand for exports and import-substitutes by increasing their output.

There is likely to be a time-lag involved between the change in price competitiveness and increased production, during which period the current balance can be expected to worsen. For this reason, governments may attempt to deflate domestic demand to release resources for export industries and to decrease the demand for imports in the initial aftermath of a currency depreciation.

3. Domestic price level

In our example, we assumed that domestic prices would be unchanged as a result of the depreciation. However, if U.K. exports have a substantial import component, the increased production of export industries would stimulate increased imports (at a higher sterling price), worsening the current balance in the short term, and increasing the costs of production (which may offset the price advantage of U.K. exports to some extent). Moreover, if import prices increase, households will face a higher cost of living, and this may be reflected in increased wage demands. If these are allowed, a wage–price spiral may result, defeating the initial price advantage gained from depreciation.

4. Non-price effects

Apart from the above factors, much will depend on the competence of U.K. firms in marketing their products and establishing new trading links, i.e. on their ability to exploit the price advantage which depreciation offers. The ability to get the right product to the right market at the right time, and to sell it against competition from established trading partners, is the key. At the same time, it is certain that foreign trading competitors will be doing everything in their power to offset the price advantage gained by U.K. exporters, and they may be supported in this by the action of their governments.

Effects on business

We have seen that under certain circumstances, floating exchange rates may bring about automatic self-adjustment in the current balance. This automatic correction avoids the need for government domestic policies aimed at maintaining a given exchange rate (which would tend to penalize exporters) and lessens the temptation to lose the benefits which trade offers by resorting to direct controls, such as import quotas. However, quite apart from the reservations expressed about their self-equilibrating nature, floating exchange rates do have disadvantages:

1. Uncertainty

There is usually a lengthy period between winning an order, supplying the goods and settling the bill. A change in the exchange rate in the interval between signing contracts and settlement may make the difference between making a profit or a loss on the deal. So it is argued that floating exchange rates may discourage trade by increasing uncertainty. This can be overcome by use of the forward exchange markets, where firms can agree to buy currency at a given future date at a contracted price.

2. Investment

It was argued above that firms would need to expand production for export if they were to take advantage of a currency depreciation. If this involves increasing capacity by undertaking investment projects, there is an obvious risk (under a floating exchange rate regime) that by the time the plant comes 'on stream' the exchange rate will be less favourable. Short-term changes in the exchange rate are obviously an inadequate basis for assessing the likely return on capital over a number of years.

3. Non-trade factors Fluctuating exchange rates are not only caused by movements in the current balance. If the government operates a tight monetary policy and interest rates rise, for example, there may be a significant inflow of hot money which raises the exchange rate. The combined effect of high interest rates, low domestic demand and increased exchange rates will present significant problems for those companies which are heavily dependent on export markets. If much effort and money has been directed to establishing a foothold in a market, the firm is faced with the dilemma of reducing profit margins to keep its prices competitive and protect its investment, or allowing its foreign prices to rise, risking the loss of foreign markets and the consequent costs of surplus domestic capacity.

4. Factor costs A fluctuating exchange rate will affect the firm's costs of production if it uses imported components. Moreover, if a depreciation is reflected in a general increase in prices in domestic markets, the firm may face increased wage demands based on the change in the cost of living.

Individual firms will be affected in different ways: what is good for some will inevitably be bad for others. For example, a rise in the exchange rate will cause problems for exporters, but importers and producers of import substitutes are likely to benefit. However, these can be seen as short-term and relatively superficial side-effects as opposed to long-term structural changes in the economy, on which international trade performance is ultimately dependent. Whilst exchange rates undoubtedly influence the pattern of trade to some extent, the stronger relationship is between the country's economic performance and its effects on trading competitiveness, of which the exchange rate is essentially a reflection.

U.K. trade performance
Whilst world trade has grown substantially in the post-war period, it is noticeable that the U.K.'s *share* of trade has fallen. Not only has the U.K.'s trade, as a proportion of national income, risen proportionately less quickly than most of its competitors, but its growth rate for national income has been poor by international standards (and therefore the growth of its trade in absolute terms has been slower). The main explanation of this is in terms of lack of competitiveness, which can be sub-divided into two categories:

1. Price competitiveness
The prices of U.K. goods are not only affected by exchange rates, but also by domestic factors:

(a) **Productive efficiency** The efficiency with which

scarce resource inputs are converted into output is fundamental to the explanation of the U.K.'s relative economic decline. It is sometimes thought that this simply means that U.K. workers do not work as hard as their counterparts in other countries.

Certainly, over-manning, absenteeism and industrial disputes will affect productivity, but there are other significant factors, most notably the level of investment (including 'investment in human capital'), and perhaps more important, the *quality* of that investment. The dimensions of the investment problem in quantitative terms can be seen from Table 8 (remembering what has previously been said about relative growth rates over the period).

Fixed investment in major industrialized countries (% of GDP)

	U.K.	France	W. Ger.	Italy	U.S.A.	Japan
Average 1950–54	14	18	20	19	17.5	21.5[1]
Average 1970–75	19	24	24	21	17.5	33.5

Table 8. Comparative levels of investment (Source: *Ibid*)
[1] average 1952–54

Investment performance will, of course, vary both between industries and between firms in the same industry, just as the quality of the investment can vary. Explanations of the U.K.'s relatively poor performance include:

– 'Vicious circle' theories: low investment is reflected in poor profitability, which therefore discourages firms from investment and so on.
– Disincentives in the tax system.
– Inadequacies in the medium-term and long-term financial markets.
– The effects of inflation.
– Adverse effects of government intervention to manage the economy.

Because of the cumulative nature both of economic growth and of technology, an initial disadvantage can be quickly exaggerated. With this in mind, many have warned of the possible long-term consequences of failure by U.K. firms to embrace the opportunities of the 'sun-rise industries'.

(b) Relative inflation rates

Allied to productive efficiency is the question of differences in rates of inflation between countries. As noted in the previous chapter, if one country has a persistently higher rate of inflation than the others, the competitiveness of its products (at home and in export markets) will decline over time. Thus, governments generally see the control of inflation as a prime objective in attempting to improve trade performance in the long run, and certainly preferrable to short-term manipulation of exchange rates.

2. Non-price competitiveness

The significance of prices should not be over-emphasized. Non-price competitiveness, which can encompass a wide range of factors such as quality, design, styling, marketing, reliability, after-sales service, delivery dates and so forth, may be just as important (although more difficult to measure precisely).

Ask someone, for example, why they bought a foreign car. It may well be that effective advertising, promotional offers, reliability, service guarantees, prompt delivery, design features and styling will feature more prominently in their answer than simply relative prices. This aspect of the 'right product in the right market at the right time' argument introduces one way of explaining the development of trade in recent years – known as the 'dynamic trade theories'.

Dynamic trade theories

The theory of comparative advantage, when combined with the existence of different resource endowments and economies of large-scale production (which are likely to result from increased specialization), suggests that international trade is likely to be beneficial, but does not really explain the development of trade in what may be classified as the same product, e.g. cars or freezers.

Product differentiation It has been argued that such trade represents an international extension of product differentiation (most notably, the non-price factors described above). Product differentiation fragments a market into separate (but inter-related) units, partly as an attempt to tailor goods more directly to the expressed wishes of a group of consumers within a larger market.

The theory is that major manufacturers in different countries will develop products which fit most closely to the preferences of domestic consumers. However, some consumers' preferences in one country may match more closely the wants of the majority of consumers in another country, so that they prefer to buy an imported good. The more segmented the market is, the greater is the likely range of imports of substitutes for the domestic manufacturer's product.

Product life-cycle In this theory there is greater emphasis on the importance of innovation and imitation. New products tend to be developed in technologically advanced, high demand, developed economies. A new product is initially launched in the domestic market, after which it is exported to other high income countries. Successful products are imitated by manufacturers in the importing country, so that these countries eventually become exporters of the product. The development of the market for the new product may result in economies of large-scale production, improved production techniques, further refinements (i.e. product differentiation), and increased competition in non-producing countries.

In the final stage of the product's life-cycle, the market is sufficiently large and the process so standardized that the lesser developed countries begin their own production. With the advantage of an established market, low relative development costs, and (often) much lower unit labour costs, these countries may, to some extent, displace the original innovators in their own markets. In the meantime, the innovative country can be expected to have progressed to new products and processes.

Whilst not being a comprehensive explanation of the development of the pattern of trade, these theories do give some insight into the way in which trade has developed in recent years, although we have identified other factors – such as relative domestic costs – which might be given more attention.

Import penetration

Table 9 gives some indication of the degree of import penetration in the U.K. market for a range of consumer durables (and to some extent illustrates the dynamic trade theories described above).

	U.K. market '000 units	Imports as % of market	Exports as % of U.K. manu-facturer's sales
Cars	1716	56	36
Telephones	1170	14	12
Television sets:			
Colour	1862	28	16
Black & white	1461	51	7
Automatic washing			
machines	1129	46	13
Tumble dryers	688	8	26
One-door refrigerators	835	31	24
Fridge-freezers	639	68	6
Vacuum cleaners	2530	46	35

Table 9. Import penetration and U.K. exports (Source: *Lloyds Bank Economic Bulletin, March 1980*)

There is no uniform pattern, but in many of the markets foreign producers have gained a considerable market share (although in some cases U.K. producers export a large part of their total output). Inevitably, increases in the market shares of importers give rise to demands from domestic manufacturers for government protection. This may take the form of quotas or tariffs, or more surreptitious forms of control through input subsidies, the manipulation of safety standards, bureaucratic delays, etc.

Protectionist arguments

Many reasons have been presented above to justify an assumption in favour of free trade, but there are some counter-arguments put forward by those desiring a protectionist strategy:

1. Infant industries It is argued that industries in the early stages of development need protection, to enable them to grow to a stage at which they are able to compete with similar industries in other countries on an equal footing. This argument is generally accepted, although there is a danger that such protection may become protracted.

2. Unfair competition This may cover a mass of alleged sins, from 'unreasonably' low wages in other countries to 'dumping' (i.e. selling goods abroad below their production cost), or concealed protection (e.g. through subsidies on inputs in foreign countries).

This is a more contentious case. However unfair the competition actually is, there is an obvious direct benefit to consumers in the form of lower prices (although, indirectly, there may be hidden costs resulting from unemployment in domestic industries and the effects of increased imports on the economy). The question then becomes one of political judgement: weighing the protection of home employment against relatively higher prices.

In the case of input subsidies and dumping, strong arguments can be put forward for protection as a means of avoiding the 'importing of other countries' unemployment'. This is particularly relevant where domestic producers are threatened with closure and there is a possibility of future import price increases to exploit the changed market situation.

3. Rationalization Industries may claim short-term protection to facilitate an orderly restructuring in the light of changed market circumstances, with a minimum of social dislocation (particularly where the industry is heavily concentrated in a particular geographical area). The dilemma here is that such protection may serve only to hinder the restructuring of the industry, and may make the economy more inflexible. There are obvious social and political overtones in such cases, e.g. shipbuilding and the steel industry in the U.K.

There are many other possible arguments, from correction of balance of payments problems to strategically significant industries, and retaliation. It is easy to confuse apparently economic arguments with social and political considerations and, indeed, a government will have to balance the microeconomic effects on particular firms with the wider macroeconomic effects of any specific measures. Just as we have argued against exchange rate manipulation as a means of influencing trade performance, so there is the danger that protectionism can be used to postpone the more fundamental structural adjustments which appear necessary to improve the U.K.'s international trade record.

Chapter 6

Market Prices

The first part of this book has been concerned with macro-economics: the study of the economy as a whole. This forms the economic environment within which individual firms set about their business, and we have observed several ways in which developments at the national level affect the activities, and impinge on the decision-making processes, of these individual enterprises. In the remaining chapters, we are primarily concerned with microeconomics: the study of the individual parts of the economy.

Markets It was noted in Chapter 1 that a market exists wherever buyers and sellers of a good or service interact, and that this does not necessarily involve direct personal contact (see page 12). Defining the limits of a market, however, is more difficult. For example, one might talk of a market for motor vehicles, but this would encompass goods as different as motor bicycles and juggernauts; even the motor car market ranges from the three-wheeler to a Rolls-Royce, which could hardly be considered to be the same good. There is no simple solution to this classification problem, but for our present purposes it is satisfactory to define a market in terms of what consumers believe to be essentially the same good, though different firms' products may vary slightly in specification or design. Thus, we can talk in terms of markets for family saloon cars, instant coffee, or colour television sets, for example, whilst recognizing that different firms' products in such markets are by no means identical.

Market prices If the products in a market are not identical, it would be surprising if the prices were. However, a change in market conditions which affects all firms equally is likely to have a similar effect, and thus it is not totally misleading to talk in terms of market prices so long as this is taken as an underlying price from which certain firms' products will deviate. We return to the question of how individual firms determine their market price and output in Chapter 8.

Market prices are formed by the interaction of demand and supply at a given time: when more is demanded at a given price than the producers are able and willing to supply, the price tends to rise; similarly, if there is excess supply, the price tends to fall. This is not universally true, since it depends on the conditions which prevail in the individual market. The most important conditions in this respect are:

1. The number of buyers and sellers The more buyers and sellers there are, the more difficult it is for any individual buyer or seller to alter the market price by his own actions. This, of course, also depends on the proportion of market output for which any one buyer or seller accounts.

2. The independence of market actors If either buyers or sellers collude, they may collectively be able to influence the market price. The more buyers or sellers there are, the more difficult it is to operate and enforce a collective strategy.

3. Degree of product differentiation The more diverse are the goods classified collectively in a single market, the more likely it is that individual products may withstand the general pressures affecting the market.

4. External constraints Prices in any market may be constrained by factors other than the wishes of the buyers and sellers. The most obvious example of this is government intervention.

Because of the number of complexities which this introduces into the analysis of market prices, economists generally base their ideas on a free market model. It is assumed that goods in the same market are identical, that there are so many buyers and sellers that no individual buyer or seller can affect the market price, and that there is no collusion and no external constraints to prevent the free interaction of demand and supply.

It is at this point that the wordly-wise businessman throws up his hands in despair or mutters about 'economics in fairyland'. What relevance can such models have to the real world which he seeks to understand? The answer is simple: a model seeks to identify and explain the underlying and fundamental aspects of a given problem. Once established, it can be used as the basis on which to test the significance of deviations from the assumptions of the model. Thus, having first considered the determination of prices in a free market in this chapter, we can proceed to an examination of the effects of government intervention in the form of indirect taxes, subsidies, buffer stocks, minimum and maximum prices and so forth. In Chapter 8, we examine the effects of relaxing the assumption about many sellers, and of introducing product differentiation or collusion. In other words, model-building is an important initial step in developing a means of analysing more specific situations: it is the economic equivalent of learning to walk before starting to run.

DEMAND

Definition The quantity of a good which consumers are able and willing to buy at a given price, in a given market, and during a given period of time, *ceteris paribus*.

The term *ceteris paribus*, meaning 'other things remaining unchanged', is the economist's equivalent of the physical scientist's laboratory. It is the intellectual means whereby he can conduct logical experiments. Again, this is not to escape from reality, but to provide a basis from which the impact of different events can be assessed. The more factors which are changing at any one time, the more difficult it is to assess the significance of changes in any individual market condition.

Motivation It is assumed that consumers buy goods and services for the satisfaction which they render, and that the aim of consumers is to get as much satisfaction as possible from a given money income.

Consumer behaviour theory

Conventional economics texts develop elaborate theories to explain why more is bought when the price falls and *vice versa*. Readers who are interested in how difficult it can become to explain the apparently obvious are referred to the 'Further Reading' section (page 118). It is useful in this context to note one important conclusion of consumer behaviour theory. This is the division of the effect of a change in price (the 'price effect') into two elements. Consider, for example, a fall in the price of one good, *ceteris paribus*. It has two simultaneous effects:

1. The substitution effect The good is now cheaper relative to the prices of other goods than it was previously. Consumer behaviour theory can demonstrate conclusively that the consumer will buy more of a good whose relative price falls, *ceteris paribus*.

2. Income effect Other things, however, do not remain equal when the relative price changes, since the fall in price also affects the consumer's *real* income. For example, the consumer could buy all the goods he chose prior to the price fall and still have money left over. Unlike the substitution effect, the income effect may incline the consumer to buy less of the good whose price has fallen, if he considers it inferior to other goods which he prefers now that his real income has risen. Alternatively, the rise in real income may incline him to buy more of the good whose price has fallen.

Price effect =Substitution effect + Income effect

Thus, the overall price effect depends on the relative strengths and the directions of these two component effects, and provides the means for categorizing goods:

Normal goods When the price of the good falls, both the substitution effect and the income effect operate in the same direction, inclining the consumer to buy more of the good.

Inferior goods When price falls, the two effects conflict: the substitution effect inclining the consumer to buy more and the income effect motivating him to buy less (and to buy more of a superior substitute). Usually, experience shows that the substitution effect is stronger than the income effect, with the net result that *the consumer buys more of the good whose price has fallen.*

Giffen goods There is an exceptional case in which the income effect not only operates in the opposite direction to the substitution effect, but outweighs it. In this case, less is bought when price falls, or more is bought when the price rises. Goods with this characteristic are termed 'Giffen goods' after the professor who first provided an explanation of this unusual phenomenon.

Giffen goods are very much the exception. They are only likely to exist where a good accounts for the major proportion of customers' expenditure, so that a change in price has a very substantial effect on real income. In some lesser developed countries, rice may be considered a Giffen good. If a peasant spends 90% of income on rice and 10% on meat, for example, a 10% fall in the price of rice will increase his real income by 9%, so that he may be able to increase his consumption of meat to the extent that he does not need to purchase so much rice. Conversely, a 10% rise in the price of rice will so decrease his real income that he may be unable to afford any meat, and so will marginally increase his purchase of rice as an inferior dietary substitute.

Demand curves

Thus, consumer behaviour theory indicates that, with the single and unlikely exception of a Giffen good, the demand for any good will rise when price falls, or will fall when price rises, provided that other factors are unchanged. This conclusion is illustrated in Figure 7, where the demand curve (D_1) slopes downwards from left to right.

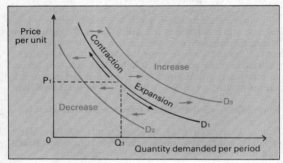

Figure 7. Demand curves

The *ceteris paribus* proviso (i.e. that other things remain unchanged) is particularly important here. If there was a sudden health scare regarding a particular product, for example, both the price and the quantity bought might fall simultaneously. But this results from a change in one of the *conditions of demand,* not from the change in price. So this event would be shown by a *shift* of the demand curve to the left, which indicates that less is demanded at *every* price.

Thus, we must be careful to distinguish between movements along the demand curve (caused by a change in price, *ceteris paribus*) and shifts of the demand curve (caused by a change in the underlying conditions of demand). This is achieved by careful use of terminology, as indicated in Figure 7:

1. Contraction Less is demanded as a result of a rise in the good's price, *ceteris paribus*.

2. Expansion (or 'extension') More is demanded as the good's price falls, *ceteris paribus*.

Both of these are indicated by a movement along the demand curve.

3. Decrease Less is demanded at every price: the whole curve shifts to the left.

4. Increase More is demanded at every price: the whole curve shifts to the right.

Both of these result from a change in the conditions of demand.

Conditions of demand

Thus, we need to identify those conditions of demand, i.e. the factors, other than the good's own price, which may affect the quantity demanded. Conventionally, three main factors are identified:

1. Prices of other goods There are two main demand relationships under this heading:

 (a) Competitive demand, where one good is a substitute for the other. For example, if the price of pork falls and more is bought, then the demand for beef would be expected to decrease (i.e. the demand curve for beef shifts to the left).

 (b) Joint demand, where one good complements the consumption of the other. For example, if the price of pork falls and more is bought, then the demand for bottled apple sauce would be expected to increase (i.e. the demand curve for apple sauce shifts to the right).

2. Incomes of consumers When consumers' incomes change, the effect on the quantity demanded will depend on the nature of the good (as indicated in consumer behaviour theory):

 (a) Inferior goods, where the income effect is negative, i.e. when incomes rise, consumers buy less of the good (and more of a superior substitute), so that the demand curve shifts to the left.

 (b) Normal goods, where the income effect is positive, i.e. when incomes rise, consumers buy more of the good at any given price, so that the demand curve shifts to the right.

3. Tastes and preferences Over time, the demand for a good may increase or decrease as a result of changing fashions, the availability of new products, health scares and so forth. Any such change will cause a shift of the demand curve.

There are many other conditions of demand which could be cited, often depending on the nature of the good, e.g. the weather. Also, consumers' expectations can be an important condition of demand; for example, the expectation of a shortage or future price rise may cause an increase in demand. In summary, a change in any factor, other than the good's own price, which affects the demand for a product is indicated by a shift of the demand curve.

Demand forecasts

In practice, firms may have a very limited range of information about the demand for their product at anything other than the existing price. They realize that the demand is not only dependent on their own actions (e.g. advertising), but also on the actions of other firms in the market. Thus, at the level of the individual firm, and particularly in the case of the launch of new products, much effort may be put into forecasting the level of demand for a given price range. Such forecasts are clearly important, since the firm has to make important decisions (e.g. the employment of labour, plant capacity and the ordering of raw materials) in anticipation of the level of demand. (These matters are considered in more detail in the *Marketing* book in this series.)

The market demand curves (such as those in Figure 7) shown here, take the form of a prediction of the quantity which consumers would be able and willing to buy if the price was at a given level. The greater the deviation from the prevailing market price, the more difficult it is to estimate the quantity demanded with any degree of precision.

SUPPLY

Definition The quantity of a good which producers are able and willing to offer for sale at a given price in a given market during a specified period of time, *ceteris paribus*.

Supply curves

Clearly, the effect of increasing output on firms' costs will exert an important influence on the quantity firms supply as price rises. We examine this aspect of supply in more detail in the following chapter. This apart, it seems likely that the higher the price, the more profitable production will become, and so the greater will be the quantity supplied. This is shown in Figure 8, which shows a supply curve, S_1, sloping upwards from left to right.

As with demand curves, we need to distinguish carefully between movements along the supply curve, which result from a change in price *ceteris paribus,* and shifts of the supply curve, which result from a change in the conditions of supply:

1. Contraction Less is supplied as a result of a fall in the good's price, *ceteris paribus*.

2. Expansion (or 'extension') More is supplied as the good's price rises, *ceteris paribus*.

Both of these are indicated by a movement along the supply curve (to the left and right respectively).

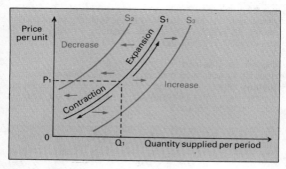

Figure 8. Supply curves

3. Decrease Less is supplied at every price: the whole curve shifts to the left.

4. Increase More is supplied at every price: the whole curve shifts to the right.

An increase or decrease in supply can result only from a change in the conditions of supply.

Conditions of supply
The conditions of supply are those factors, other than changes in the good's own price, which may affect the quantity supplied. There are many such conditions, of which those most commonly cited include:

1. Factor prices A change in factor prices will alter the firms' costs of production and hence their profitability, *ceteris paribus*. For example, an increase in wage-rates would be expected to cause a decrease in supply.

2. Number of firms If more firms enter an industry, supply would be expected to increase at every given price; conversely supply would decrease if firms left an industry.

3. Technology Changes in the efficiency with which the firms can convert factor inputs into output will also affect profitability, *ceteris paribus*. Thus, improved technology would be expected to cause an increase in supply.

Other conditions of supply include changes in the objectives of firms, changes in the prices and profitability of other products, government policy and the discovery of new (or exhaustion of existing) raw materials.

Time The ability to alter the quantity supplied depends on the time period under consideration. For example, where a product has a lengthy production cycle (e.g. agricultural products), or where existing productive capacity is already stretched, no significant change in the quantity supplied may be possible in the short run even for big price rises. The question of the responsiveness of the quantity supplied to a change in price – the 'price elasticity of supply' – is considered further in the next chapter.

Market equilibrium

Since we have related both the quantity demanded and the quantity supplied to the good's own price, we can super-impose a demand curve and a supply curve on a single diagram, as in Figure 9.

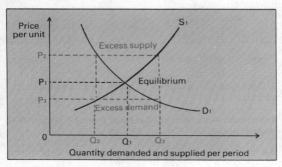

Figure 9. Market equilibrium

There is only one price (P_1) and only one quantity (Q_1) at which the plans of consumers and producers are exactly matched, and the market is 'cleared'. This is known as the 'market equilibrium': where the quantity demanded is equal to the quantity supplied at a given price, in a given market and during a given time period, *ceteris paribus*.

Excess supply If the price were P_2, the quantity supplied would exceed the quantity demanded by the amount, $Q_3 - Q_2$, i.e. there is excess supply. In a free market, competition between the producers to reduce their unsold stocks would force the price downwards, causing an extension of demand. As price falls, so the supply curve shows that the quantity supplied will contract. The process continues until the market equilibrium is achieved.

Excess demand A similar argument applies if the price were below the equilibrium, at P_3. In this case, there is excess demand equal to $Q_3 - Q_2$, and competition between consumers to get the good will push the price upwards, inducing an expansion of supply and a contraction of demand until the market equilibrium is again achieved.

This demonstrates that, given a free market based on the assumptions cited, there is an in-built automatic mechanism to maintain market equilibrium. We can extend this argument to show how the price mechanism restores equilibrium in the event of a change in one of the conditions of demand or supply.

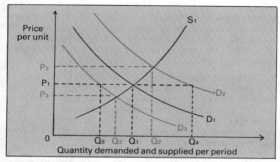

Figure 10. Changes in the conditions of demand

In each of the four examples below (referring to Figures 10 and 11), we assume an initial equilibrium at OP_1, OQ_1.

1. Increased demand This might be caused, for example, by an increase in consumer incomes for a normal good, *ceteris paribus*. The demand curve shifts to the right (to D_2). At the original equilibrium price of OP_1, there would now be excess demand equal to $OQ_4 - OQ_1$ as shown in Figure 10. Competition between consumers forces the price upwards, inducing an expansion of supply and contraction of demand along D_2 until a new equilibrium is achieved at OP_2, OQ_2: both the price and the quantity exchanged have thus increased.

2. Decreased demand Conversely, if demand decreases to D_3 in Figure 10 (perhaps because of the introduction of a new substitute good), there will be excess supply of $OQ_1 - OQ_5$ at OP_1, so that competition between producers will force the price down, inducing an expansion of demand along D_3 until the new equilibrium is established at OP_3, OQ_3. In this case, both price and quantity exchanged fall.

3. Increased supply In Figure 11, if supply is increased to

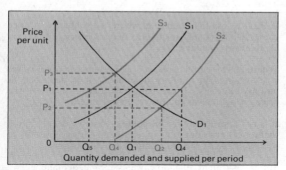

Figure 11. Changes in the conditions of supply

S₂ (e.g. as a result of decreased factor costs), there will be
excess supply at OP₁ equal to OQ₄ − OQ₁. Competition
between producers to sell their surplus stocks will result
eventually in the formation of a new equilibrium at OP₂,
OQ₂. Whilst the price has fallen (compared with the original
equilibrium), the quantity exchanged has risen.

4. Decreased supply If supply decreases to S₃ in Figure 11
(as a result of some firms leaving the industry, for example),
there will be excess demand at the original equilibrium price
of OP₁. Competition between the consumers will bring
about a new equilibrium at OP₃, OQ₄, demonstrating that,
in comparison with the original equilibrium, price has risen
and the quantity exchanged has fallen.

An important result from these observations is that movements along one curve result from changes in the market
conditions affecting the other curve, i.e. a movement along
the demand curve results from a change in the conditions of
supply, and a movement along the supply curve is brought
about by a change in the conditions of demand.

ELASTICITY

We have seen that a shift of the supply curve will cause a
movement along the demand curve, and will usually alter
both the price and the quantity exchanged. From the firms'
point of view, the extent of these changes is very important
since it will affect the amount of money received from
selling their output (i.e. their total revenue).

Price elasticity of demand (PED) is defined as the
responsiveness of the quantity demanded to a change in
price in a given market, during a given time period, *ceteris
paribus*. It can be measured using the following equation:

$$\text{PED} = \frac{\text{Percentage change in quantity demanded}}{\text{Percentage change in price}}$$

If PED is greater than one (e.g. where a 1% change in price
causes a 2% change in quantity demanded), it is described as
'relatively elastic'.

If PED is less than one (e.g. where a 1% change in price
causes a 0.5% change in quantity demanded), it is described
as 'relatively inelastic'.

Where PED is equal to one (i.e. a 1% change in price causes
a 1% change in quantity demanded) it is described as
'unitary elasticity'. It can be shown that, in this case, the
price change leaves total revenue unaltered.

It is not appropriate in this context to delve deeply into a
theoretical consideration of elasticity, but it is useful to
present some of the more important conclusions:

1. For a straight line downward-sloping demand curve,
PED will be different at every point. This is because PED

depends not only on the slope of the demand curve, but also on the ratio of the original price and quantity.

2. There are three demand curves with constant elasticity along their length: horizontal (PED = ∞), vertical (PED = 0), and where the demand curve forms a rectangular hyperbola (unitary elasticity).

3. If demand is relatively elastic, a price fall causes total revenue to rise, and a price rise causes total revenue to fall, i.e. price and total revenue move in opposite directions.

If demand is relatively inelastic, a price fall causes total revenue to fall, and a price rise causes total revenue to rise, i.e. price and total revenue change in the same direction.

Applications of PED

1. Revenue changes As indicated above, PED is useful in measuring the effect on revenue of changes in price.

2. Clearance sales When a certain amount of stock has to be cleared within a given period, knowledge of PED will be useful in estimating the percentage decrease in price which would be required to induce the necessary percentage expansion of demand: the danger being that too great a price reduction will result in forgone profits, and too small a reduction will fail to clear the stock.

3. Exchange rate changes We have previously shown that since changes in the exchange rate alter the relative prices of imports and exports, PED is important in calculating the effect on the net currency flow (see p.68).

4. Indirect taxes If the Chancellor wishes to increase tax revenue by increasing taxes, he will need to impose the tax on goods with relatively inelastic demand. If he seeks to discourage consumption of goods (e.g. imports through the imposition of tariffs) he will be more successful where demand is relatively elastic.

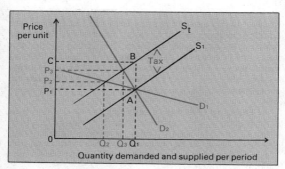

Figure 12. Indirect taxes and price

In Figure 12, the original equilibrium is where price is equal to OP_1 and the quantity exchanged is OQ_1. We can take point A on the supply curve as representing the producers' desire for a total revenue, shown by the area OP_1AQ_1, if they are to make this quantity available. Thus, if a tax equal to AB per unit were imposed on the good, the price would need to rise to OC if they were to retain the same revenue (after the government has taken its tax revenue) for selling the same quantity. For this reason, we show the imposition of a tax by raising the supply curve at every level of output by the amount of the tax: to S_t in Figure 12.

However, this does not mean that the firms actually receive the unchanged revenue, since it can be seen that a rise in price causes a contraction of demand: hence the significance of PED in predicting the effects of indirect tax changes. In Figure 12, two demand curves are shown for the purpose of comparison. Since the original price and quantity are the same at A, the slopes of the demand curves show the relative price elasticities: over the price range P_1 to P_3, D_1 is more elastic than D_2. It can be seen that the more inelastic the demand curve is, the less the effect on the quantity exchanged and the greater the proportion of the tax which is passed on to the consumer in the form of higher prices.

Price controls
In some markets, prices may not be free to react to the forces of demand and supply. This may result from government intervention, for example, or because prices are administered by a central body.

1. Maximum prices
Perhaps the most common form of control is when price is prevented from rising beyond a stated value. This is usually intended as a form of consumer protection: to enable some consumers to buy the good or service who would otherwise be priced out of the market, e.g. rent controls or Cup Final tickets. Alternatively, the intention may be linked to controlling inflation or preventing suppliers from making what are considered excessive profits during a temporary shortage.

Clearly, if the maximum price is above the free market equilibrium price, it will have no direct effect. However, referring back to Figure 10 (page 83), we can see that if a maximum price was set at OP_3, a situation of excess demand would prevail without the traditional means of restoring equilibrium (i.e. price). There are several possible consequences of such a situation:

(a) **Queuing** One way of resolving excess demand is to form queues, whether these consist of waiting lists (e.g. for Council houses) or lines of people outside retail outlets. These are normally formed on a 'first come, first served' basis, but some criteria for priority treatment may be incorporated.
(b) **Rationing** Prices and queues are in themselves a form

of rationing the available supply between competing consumers. Other forms of rationing may be determined by the sellers (e.g. preference to regular customers or limits to the quantity which any one consumer may buy) or by a central authority, such as the government, which may use a coupon system to limit the quantity purchased by each consumer.

(c) Hoarding One perverse consequence of a shortage is that people may actually increase their purchase to lessen the possibility of being 'caught short'; this shifts the demand curve to the right and exacerbates the situation.

(d) Loopholes If consumers are prepared to pay a price higher than the minimum, and suppliers are prepared to sell greater quantities at a higher price, there is a mutual advantage in finding legitimate means of circumventing the maximum price. For example, the controlled good may be 'given away' with an uncontrolled product sold at a much inflated price.

(e) Black market For the same reason that legitimate loopholes are sought, others may be prepared simply to break the price control regulations, in which case the price would be likely to be higher than the free market equilibrium prices. For example, in Figure 9, if supply was limited to OQ_2, the market would be cleared at a price of OP_2.

(f) Supply effects On the supply side, the production of substitute goods (whose prices are not controlled) may be stimulated, which may have the effect of reducing the excess demand for the controlled good.

There is no reason to expect that the supply of the controlled good will increase to remove the excess demand and form an equilibrium at the maximum price. However, the body imposing the maximum price may take measures at the same time either to decrease demand or to increase supply. In general, maximum prices can be expected to leave unfulfilled demand: in Figure 9, the quantity $OQ_1 - OQ_2$ which would have been exchanged in a free market, or the quantity $OQ_3 - OQ_2$ which is demanded at the maximum price. Those consumers successful in buying the desired quantity at the maximum price benefit (although time spent queuing may counteract this) but those who would have bought at OP_1 but cannot at OP_3 may well feel ill-treated (particularly if the aim of the price control was consumer protection).

Subsidies

An alternative means of removing the excess demand, if the government has instituted the maximum price, is to grant subsidies to producers. Diagrammatically these have the opposite effect to indirect taxes (see Figure 12): the supply curve shifts downwards by the amount of the subsidy at every given level of output. Whilst restoring equilibrium, there are obvious redistributive effects to be considered (i.e. who ultimately pays for the subsidies and who benefits), as well as the wider macroeconomic implications for the PSBR, the level of aggregate monetary demand and so forth.

2. Minimum prices

A minimum price set below the market equilibrium will not affect the market price. There are, however, examples where agreed minimum prices (e.g. international air fares) leave excess supply. In terms of Figure 10, a minimum price of OP_2 would result in excess supply of $OQ_3 - OQ_2$. The possible consequences of this situation include:

(a) **Decreased supply** This situation does have a self-equilibriating mechanism (which probably accounts for it being less common than maximum prices). If firms in the industry have unsold stocks and cannot remove them by lowering price, they may be forced to leave the industry, so that eventually supply might decrease to the extent that it intersects with D_1 at OQ_2, forming a market equilibrium at the minimum price. If the scheme was intended to protect producers – the usual reason – those forced out of business would probably consider it unsuccessful.

(b) **Loopholes** Suppliers with spare capacity might find various ways of circumventing the minimum price, e.g. 'giving away' other goods or services with the controlled product (to form an effective discount) or other forms of surreptitious price decrease.

The minimum price may be accompanied by measures designed to increase demand (e.g. advertising) in an attempt to reduce the excess supply and create an equilibrium at OP_2, OQ_3.

Buffer stock schemes

A system of price controls may be used in conjunction with a buffer stock scheme. If market price would otherwise fall below the minimum price, the central agency buys up excess supplies at the minimum price and adds these to its buffer stock. If the market price rises to the maximum, goods are released from the buffer stock at the maximum price. Between these limits, the market price prevails.

Buffer stocks are most commonly adopted for agricultural products, since supply tends to fluctuate from year to year, or because geographically concentrated social groups are highly dependent on income from agricultural goods. Other reasons include the desire to ensure continuity of supply and to protect consumers from excessive price fluctuations. To be successful, a buffer stock scheme must have total control over supply in a region. If the minimum price is set too high, stocks may become unduly high, with resultant storage costs or wastage.

Chapter 7

Costs of Production

Production is the process in which factor inputs are converted into goods and services. In this chapter, we are concerned primarily with the efficiency of this process, and the effect on a firm's costs of changing the size of its output. The production process itself, from the planning and development stage through to plant maintenance (and including the factors influencing the location of firms), is considered in far more detail than is possible here in the *Production* title in this series.

The division of labour

It is no coincidence that Adam Smith's great work, *'The Wealth of Nations'*, commences with a discussion of specialization by individual workers within the production process (i.e. 'the division of labour') and that this is also a central theme of *'The Communist Manifesto'* by Marx and Engels. Needless to say, the two books come to very different conclusions on the virtues of this phenomenon, but both acknowledge it to be one of the most significant developments in the history of man's relationship with his environment. The division of labour is the basis of industrial society as we know it (both in capitalist and communist countries).

Advantages When compared with a system in which each worker is individually responsible for the complete production of a good, a production line incorporating the principle of the division of labour has the following advantages:

1. Natural aptitudes Some workers will be better than others at different aspects of the production process. The division of labour can take advantage of these differing natural aptitudes by allowing workers to specialize in those activities at which they are more efficient. This idea is explained formally by the principle of comparative advantage: on page 63, simply substitute 'process' for 'good', and 'worker' for 'country' in the tables explaining the principle.

2. Learning Repetition of a single task will reinforce the comparative advantage of the worker. Practice may not make perfect, but it can certainly improve both the speed and quality of a worker's output. Also, individual tasks are learned more quickly than the entire production process.

3. Overheads Where several workers are each completing the whole production process, a significant amount of duplication of equipment may be necessary (to prevent waiting for tools or machines to be available). Such overhead costs may be considerably reduced where each worker only needs the equipment for one aspect of the production process.

4. Time-saving Apart from the time-savings accomplished on the tooling side, a production line removes the need for the worker to move with the part-finished product between machines appropriate to specific stages of the good's construction.

The division of labour can also be applied to the management function, so that specialists in accountancy and finance, production control, personnel work, marketing and so forth can be expected to be more efficient than managers attempting to perform several roles, provided that such ·specialists are used to capacity.

Moreover, specialization may be applied to the capital equipment used by the firm. This may simplify certain tasks in terms of required labour skills, and may further reduce labour training time, as well as increasing the productive efficiency of each worker.

Disadvantages The use of the division of labour (and more significantly, *how* it is used) can have disadvantages:

1. Job satisfaction Workers who see only one aspect of a product's construction may take little satisfaction in the quality and reliability of the end product. This may result in a higher level of reject or sub-standard goods, when compared with individual responsibility for the complete process, with concomitant costs in terms of wasted materials and labour and machine time.

2. Boredom Constant repetition of a simple manual operation may lead to boredom, which may give rise to costly 'pranks' intended to enliven the working day, or may make workers over-sensitive to minor changes or problems, resulting in petty disputes with management. On the other hand, the repetitive nature of the work may be thought a positive advantage by some employees: for example, if it provides the opportunity for conversation whilst working.

3. Disruptive potential The division of labour increases the interdependence of workers. If a group of workers at one stage of the production process goes on strike, it may not be long before the whole production line has seized up, and this can have effects on production in components firms and suppliers of raw materials, as well as on the distributors. Where labour is organized, this disruptive potential is a significant bargaining advantage for employees.

4. Inflexibility The nature of a production line is such that products need to be standardized (within certain limits) and this may make firms less able to meet the specific requirements of individual customers.

Recognition of such disadvantages is the first step in overcoming the associated problems. For example, some firms have used production teams who work together to complete the good, and others make a point of allowing workers to change from one task to another at intervals. Whilst there are obviously limits to the extent to which it is advisable to take the principle, there can be no doubt that the division of labour greatly increases the productive capacity of workers, and thereby greatly increases their earnings and material living standards.

SHORT RUN COSTS

The short run, in economics, is defined as the period in which at least one of the factors of production is in fixed supply. These fixed costs (or 'overheads') might include, for example, contracted commitments to rent or salaries, or interest on long-term loans. Similarly, it may take time to increase certain factors, for example, acquiring new factories or machines. The existence of fixed factors means that:

1. The firm will have some costs in the short run, whether it produces or not.

2. The scale of the firm's production is fixed in the short run, although it can change the level of its output by altering those factors which are variable.

3. The more the firm produces, the lower its average fixed costs will be. This is often termed 'spreading overheads'.

Law of diminishing returns
We can illustrate the limitations imposed by the existence of fixed factors by means of a simple example. Imagine a manufacturing company with a fixed factory space and a given set of capital equipment. These factors are fixed, and the only other factor required to produce the good is labour. We could observe the effect on output of increasing the number of workers employed in the factory (assuming each individual worker to be of equal ability). We would obviously expect output to increase per period as more workers are added, but it is the *rate* at which output increases which is important.

At first, the addition of extra workers might cause the rate of increased output to rise as a result of the benefits of the division of labour. However, the law of diminishing returns predicts that: *as successive identical units of a variable factor are added to a fixed quantity of other factors, there will come a point where each additional amount of output is less than that added by the previous unit of input.* In other words, output will (after some point) increase at a decreasing rate. This results from the limitations exerted by the fixed factors, e.g. limited work space and limited amounts of capital equipment in our example.

Marginal product is defined as the change in output resulting from a small change in the variable input. Thus, the law of diminishing returns predicts that after some point marginal product will start to fall and continue to do so as additional units of the variable factor are added. Given marginal product, if we know the cost of each unit of variable input, we can calculate by how much costs will rise as output is changed.

Marginal cost (MC) is the change in total cost resulting from a small change in output.

Since only one factor is variable in our example, the only cause of a change in costs must be a change in variable input. The law of diminishing returns, therefore, not only shows that (after some point) marginal product falls, but also that (at the same point) marginal costs start to rise, since successively greater amounts of variable input are needed to achieve each extra unit of output.

Short run cost curves

The production function shows the relationship between inputs of the different factors and output. With knowledge of the cost of each of these factors, we can construct a diagram showing the costs associated with different levels of output.

Total variable cost (TVC) is the total expenditure on those factors of production which can be changed in the short run, such as labour and raw materials.

Average variable cost (AVC) is simply TVC divided by the level of output (Q).

Total fixed cost (TFC) is the total expenditure on fixed factors of production (discussed above).

Average fixed cost (AFC) is TFC divided by the level of output (Q).

Total costs (TC) equal TVC plus TFC.

Average total costs (ATC) can be found either by adding AFC and AVC for any level of output, or by dividing TC by Q.

Figure 13 shows the marginal and average cost curves which are derived from the cost schedule below:

OUTPUT (per day)	TC £	MC £	AFC £	AVC £	ATC £
0	200	–	–	–	–
1	222	22	200.0	22	222.0
2	232	10	100.0	16	116.0
3	236	4	66.7	12	78.7
4	240	4	50.0	10	60.0
5	250	10	40.0	10	50.0
6	272	22	33.3	12	45.3
7	312	40	28.6	16	44.6
8	376	64	25.0	22	47.0
9	470	94	22.2	30	52.2
10	600	130	20.0	40	60.0

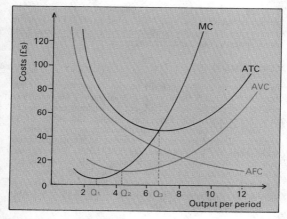

Figure 13. Cost curves

In the table, marginal cost is calculated for each additional unit of output produced, and is therefore plotted midway between two units in the diagram. Thus, the MC for an increase in output from 4 to 5 units (£10) is plotted at 4.5 units.

Since these cost curves are used extensively in the next chapter, it is important to grasp a clear understanding of their inter-relationship:

1. Diminishing returns to a factor set in at the point where marginal costs start to rise: output OQ_1.

2. Optimum output Production is most efficient in the short run at the output where ATC is at its minimum. The optimum output in Figure 13 is OQ_3.

3. Marginal and average costs The MC curve cuts both the AVC and ATC curves at their lowest points (and hence the optimum output is where ATC = MC). The usual analogy is with cricket scores: for the average to rise, each extra (or 'marginal') innings must be greater than the previous average, and for the average to fall the marginal innings must be less than the average. Only when the marginal innings is equal to the average, is the average unchanged: this is indicated by the flat slope at the bottom of the ATC curve.

4. Average total costs fall rapidly as the fixed costs are spread over a larger output, but eventually this is counteracted by rising AVC caused by diminishing returns. Between output OQ_2 and OQ_3, ATC is falling although AVC is rising. This is because AFC is falling faster than AVC is rising; beyond OQ_3, AVC rises faster than AFC falls, and so ATC rises.

5. Since ATC = AVC + AFC, the vertical distance at any output between ATC and AVC must equal AFC. For this reason, it is not usually considered necessary to show AFC as a separate cost curve in diagrams.

LONG RUN COSTS

In the short run, the scale of production is limited by the existence of fixed factors. In the long run, all factors of production can be varied (subject to constant technology). In other words, the firm can change the scale of its production. Having chosen a particular scale, its output will again be limited by the fixed factors appropriate to that scale. Thus, the long run average cost (LRAC) can be seen as a decision-making curve, enclosing the different possible scales of operation which the firm can choose between. In Figure 14, the LRAC shows the least-cost method of producing any given level of output, assuming three possible scales of output open to the firm.

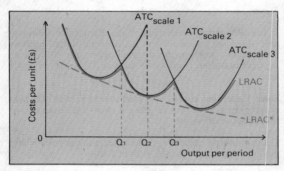

Figure 14. Long run average cost curve

It can be seen from Figure 14 that, in the long run, there are alternative ways of producing any given output. For example, the least cost method of producing output OQ_2 is where the firm chooses to produce at 'scale 2'. The same output could be produced at 'scale 1', but at a much greater unit cost (whereas scale 1 would result in lower unit costs than scale 2 for outputs less than OQ_1). At scale 2, the firm operates with *spare capacity* if it produces less than OQ_2, and *'beyond capacity'* if it produces more than OQ_2. In the former case, overheads are being spread over too small an output to achieve maximum efficiency and, in the latter case, the fixed factors exert an increasingly costly constraint (as a result of diminishing returns to the variable factors) as output is increased.

LRAC has an irregular slope because of the limited number of possible scales open to the firm in our example. If there were an infinite range of different productive scales, and we again joined the least cost methods of producing each output, we would derive a smooth downward-sloping curve as shown by LRAC* in Figure 14. This might level out at some point but (given the assumption that all factors are variable) would not be expected to rise again. The idea that average costs fall as output is increased in the long run is described as increasing returns to scale, or simply 'economies of scale'.

Economies of scale
There are several complementary factors which can cause long run average costs to fall as the scale of production is increased.

1. Technical economies
The most obvious technical economy deriving from a larger scale of production is the extension of the division of labour. This may be complemented by the use of more specialized equipment at different stages of the production process, which could not be used to capacity if a smaller scale of production existed.

The **minimum efficient plant size** (MEPS) is defined by the scale of production at which average costs would fall by less than 5% if output were doubled. If the MEPS is high relative to the output in an industry, then large-scale production is necessary if production is to be efficient. Relative to U.K. sales, the MEPS is estimated at about 10% for potato crisps, 30% for electric cookers and over 75% for tractors, for example.

Where a production line involves a series of machines with different capacities, the larger enterprise is more likely to be able to gain a technical economy by combining the machines in such numbers as to ensure a capacity through-put. The ratio of machines would be determined by the lowest common multiple of their respective outputs.

Other technical economies may be achieved by spreading the costs of research, and those of development and design, over greater quantities of output, linking productive processes that would otherwise be carried on by separate firms, or being able to take commercial advantage of by-products.

2. Managerial economies
This is an extension of the division of labour to the management function. Larger enterprises can employ (and use to capacity) specialist managers, whose skill enhances the productive efficiency of different aspects of the firm. A smaller enterprise might either use such specialists below their productive capacity, or may require them to assist in areas where their specialist skills are inappropriate.

3. Financial economies
Generally, larger organizations have more ready access to credit and loans, and at a lower cost, than smaller enterprises. This is explained in detail in the *Finance* book in this series.

4. Risk-bearing economies

Large firms are more likely to be able to protect themselves
from changes in market conditions. They might achieve this
through:

(a) **Brand proliferation** Introducing different brands of
what is essentially the same product (e.g. washing
powders) fragments the market. A new firm may make
in-roads on one section of an established firm's market,
whilst leaving other related brands relatively unaffected.

(b) **Product diversification** The commercial equivalent
of not putting all your eggs in one basket. By operating in
several markets, the firm is less exposed in the event of
set-backs in any individual market.

(c) **Product development** There are obvious costs in
developing and launching new products. The large firm
can spread its development and marketing costs over a
wider range of new products, so that individual failures
have a less devastating effect on the overall commercial
security of the firm.

5. Commercial and marketing economies

There are various other advantages of large-scale
production which are less easily classified, but include:

(a) **Bargaining power** Relatively small suppliers, in
particular, may be dependent on the large firm's custom
for their survival. This gives the large firm significant
strength in agreeing favourable prices.

(b) **Bulk-buying** Large orders generally justify a discount
since there are economies involved in selling large
quantities to one firm rather than small quantities to
many smaller firms. For example, the supplier's sales
costs, packaging and invoicing, and transport costs (per
unit sold) are invariably lower.

(c) **Advertising** Large firms can promote their products
regularly and on a national scale, reducing the unit sales
costs. By promoting a company name or image in
association with one product line, the sales of other
product lines produced by the same company are likely to
be cross-fertilized (e.g. *Heinz* '57 varieties').

There is insufficient space here to amplify these economies,
but readers are referred to the *Marketing* title in this series
for further discussion of the topic.

Diseconomies of scale

It has been suggested that the LRAC will *not* slope upwards
as the scale of production increases. This is based on the
assumption that in the long run all factors are variable and
that perfect mobility exists in the factor market. If these
assumptions do not hold, unit factor costs, for example,
might increase as a result of excess demand as the scale of
production increased. Alternatively, if production becomes
more intensely geographically concentrated, unit
distribution costs are likely to rise (but are unlikely to
outweigh the other economies gained).

Managerial diseconomies It is often argued that large-scale enterprises may suffer diseconomies as a result of the difficulties involved in co-ordinating the decision-making and production processes. This really means that the managerial function imposes a constraint on the size of businesses, and the validity of this ultimately revolves around the quality of managerial skills.

Experience

The very long run, in economics, is defined as the period in which all factors are variable; the production process is subject to the benefits of new technology and learning as well as scale: collectively termed 'experience'. As experience of producing a new product is gained over time, unit production costs can be expected to fall, and this is likely to be reflected in real prices. The pocket calculator provides a staggering example of the effects of experience, both in terms of unit production costs and quality. The greater the initial costs of research and development, the more dramatic the effects of experience are likely to be.

Elasticity of supply

The price elasticity of supply (PES) measures the responsiveness of the quantity supplied to a change in price in a given market during a given period of time, *ceteris paribus*.

$$PES = \frac{\text{Percentage change in quantity supplied per period}}{\text{Percentage change in price}}$$

One important application of the PES was considered when discussing the effects of changes in the exchange rate on a country's international currency flow (see page 68). The factors which influence PES include:

1. Time is probably the most significant influence on PES. In the immediate time period, the response to a rise in price is limited by the stocks of the firms in the industry. In the short run, production can be increased by increasing the input of variable factors, but this will affect unit costs: if the firm has spare capacity, unit costs will decrease, but if it is already at or beyond capacity, unit costs will rise (in which case PES will be lower and will depend on the rate at which unit costs increase relative to increased output).

PES in the long run is likely to be higher for most goods than in the short run, since firms can alter their scale of production. However, firms will only expand their scale of production if they are confident that the change in price is likely to be permanent (especially where overhead costs are high).

2. Specific factors The chronological length of the long run varies enormously between different markets. If price rises and the firm decides to expand its productive scale by new investment, there will be a **gestation** period before these plans come to fruition. The length of this period depends to a large extent on how specific the investment is to a particular production process. Where the producer good is standardized the gestation period may be very short, but if it has to be tailored to the specific requirements of the firm, the gestation period will tend to be longer.

3. Production cycle The duration of the production cycle is another important influence on the PES of a good. For example, the rise in world oil prices following the OPEC agreement in 1973 stimulated the search for new sources of supply. However, the exploration and construction period is lengthy (partly because of the need for highly specific investment goods), so that the supply adjustment would be measured in years rather than weeks.

The length of the production cycle is also particularly relevant in the case of agricultural products for obvious reasons. In these cases, the ease with which resources can be transferred from one use to another (i.e. 'factor mobility') is also important, e.g. converting a field from pasture to arable use.

4. Cost of attracting new factors In order to increase production in the event of a rise in product price, firms will increase their demand for factors, which is likely to raise their price in the short run. This obviously affects production costs, and will therefore influence the PES.

5. New entrants The ease with which new firms can enter a market in response to a change in price will also affect the PES. This may be influenced by such factors as the minimum efficient plant size relative to industry output, the degree of brand loyalty of consumers, etc.

The degree of a price increase may be sufficiently great as to make new methods of production viable, e.g. the development of North Sea oil production. This will usually involve a considerable time-lag in the supply adjustment.

Small firms
The emphasis in this chapter has been on the advantages of large-scale production. Nevertheless, small firms retain an important role within the economy in terms of creating new employment opportunities, as suppliers of components and specialist services to larger firms, and as innovators in production techniques and product development. It is important to note the limitations to the growth of firms, and the reasons why small firms predominate in some markets.

The Bolton Committee on small firms (1971) defined small firms in manufacturing industry (for statistical purposes) as those with 200 employees or less. This applies to about 95% of U.K. manufacturing firms, representing 18% of net output and 22% of employment in the sector. Firms may remain small for a number of reasons, which include:

1. The size of the market The extent of the division of labour which is possible is limited by market demand. If total demand is low, or the market is localized, large-scale production would be inefficient.

2. Nature of the product The small firm is at an advantage where flexibility and short production runs to the specific requirements of individual customers are necessary.

3. Minimum efficient plant size (MEPS) Where the MEPS is low, relative to the size of the market, small firms may be able to compete on equal terms with large ones.

4. Entrepreneurial objectives Small firms are often associated with close control by their owners. Some owners may seek to retain this close control and to avoid the risks and stress involved in expansion. Alternatively, the entrepreneur may lack the skill to perceive the opportunity for expansion, or may prove incapable of securing the necessary additional financial resources.

At any given time, some small firms will be in the process of growth: the small firm sector is often referred to as the 'seed-bed' of the large scale enterprises of the future. Successive governments (of different political complexions) have acknowledged the importance of the small firm sector, and have made some efforts to increase their number (by providing advisory services) and to ease their specific problems (by simplifying bureaucratic requirements) trying to make funds for investment more accessible and providing some tax concessions.

The deep recession of the early 1980s in the U.K. brought about a surprising stimulus to the small firm sector. Some large corporations which closed plants (such as the British Steel Corporation) gave positive encouragement to their ex-employees to use redundancy payments to establish small businesses. They were not only able to provide factory space, but to give assistance with expert advice in specialist areas such as accountancy and law. These services were provided on a commercial basis, using the Corporation's spare capacity, and seem to have proved mutually advantageous.

Chapter 8

Theory of the Firm

The purpose of the theory of the firm is to predict the prices which firms will charge for their products and the quantity they will produce in a given period.

Revenue
As has previously been stated, the total revenue (TR) of a firm is calculated by multiplying the quantity sold (Q) by the price (P).

Average revenue (AR) is the amount the firm receives for each unit of output which is sold, i.e. the price. Since an AR curve shows the price for any quantity sold, and a demand curve shows the quantity sold for any price, they are the same thing: the AR curve = the demand curve.

Marginal revenue (MR) is the change in total revenue for a small change in output.

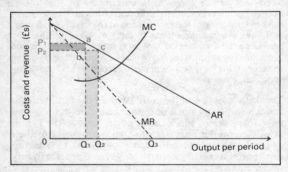

Figure 15. Marginal revenue and marginal costs

In Figure 15, to increase sales by one unit from OQ_1 to OQ_2, the firm has to reduce its price from OP_1 to OP_2. Whilst it gains revenue equal to the paler shaded area (Q_1bcQ_2 = price or average revenue), it loses revenue shown by the darker shaded area (P_2P_1ab: the reduction in price of units which were already being sold each period). We conclude that:

1. If the paler shaded area is greater than the darker shaded area, total revenue increases.
2. Average revenue (the paler shaded area) for any level of output is always greater than marginal revenue (the paler area minus the darker area).
3. If marginal revenue is positive, a small fall in price causes total revenue to rise, i.e. PED is greater than one (see page 84). At output OQ_3, total revenue is unchanged for a small fall in price (i.e. unitary PED), and at outputs greater than OQ_3 demand is relatively inelastic.

4. It can be shown that the MR curve bisects the horizontal distance between the AR curve and the vertical axis: a point to remember in constructing diagrams!

Profits

Normally, profits are thought of as the surplus of revenue over outlay. Economists take a different view: since enterprise is a productive factor, it will only be supplied at a price (because it has an opportunity cost).

Normal profits are defined as the return to enterprise just sufficient to retain it in its present use. An entrepreneur earning less than normal profits will, in the long run, take his services elsewhere. As such, normal profits constitute a cost of the firm: if it is not met, the firm closes down in the long run. Therefore, *normal profits are included in the total costs of the firm.*

Supernormal profits are the positive difference between total revenue and total costs (which include normal profits).

Profit maximization In the traditional theories of the firm, the entrepreneur's objective is assumed to be profit maximization. In Figure 15, at outputs less than OQ_2 each additional unit sold adds more to revenue than to costs (since $MR > MC$), and therefore adds to profits (or reduces losses). At outputs greater than OQ_2, each additional unit sold adds more to costs than to revenue ($MC > MR$) and thus decreases profits (or increases losses). So it can be seen that output OQ_2, where marginal cost is equal to marginal revenue, is the point at which profits are maximized (or losses are minimized). This is termed the **equilibrium output** of the firm.

Losses

It was stated above that in the long run, if the firm does not earn normal profits (or more), it will cease production. This is described as the **long run shut-down point**.

In the short run, the situation is complicated by the existence of fixed factors, which must be paid for whether the firm produces or not. Take the following example: a firm has fixed costs of £50000 and (at its equilibrium output of 10000 units) variable costs of £30000. If it can sell all of its output at £4 per unit, should it continue producing in the short run?

The firm's total costs are £80000 and its revenue (if it continues producing in the short run) is £40000: a loss of £40000. But if the firm closed down immediately, it would still have to meet its fixed costs of £50000 (and obviously would gain no revenue). Clearly, the firm (given this undesirable choice) would prefer to lose £40000 rather than £50000, and so would continue producing in the short run. If the cost and revenue conditions remain unchanged, it would close down as soon as it could discharge its fixed factors.

Thus, we derive the rule for the short run shut-down point: *a firm will cease production in the short run if its total revenue is less than its total variable costs.* (Indeed, even where this is the case, the firm may continue producing if it expects market price to rise in the near future.)

Equilibrium price and output

We have completed all the analysis necessary to determine the equilibrium price and output of any profit maximizing or loss minimizing firm. The procedure, given a graph showing the firm's cost and revenue curves, is as follows:

1. Output First, find the output at which MC = MR.
2. Price Second, from the demand (AR) curve, find the price at which this quantity will be bought.
3. Profits Finally, at the equilibrium output, compare the firm's AR and ATC:

    (a) If AR > ATC, the firm is earning supernormal profits.
    (b) If AR = ATC, the firm is earning normal profits.
    (c) If AR < ATC, the firm is earning less than normal profits: if AR ⩾ AVC the firm will continue producing in the short run, otherwise, it will cease production immediately.

Imperfect markets

In traditional theory, any market in which a firm has a downward-sloping demand curve is considered 'imperfect' (since the firm could increase its price without losing all its customers to other firms). In Figure 16, we apply the procedure described above to find the equilibrium price and output for a firm in an imperfect market.

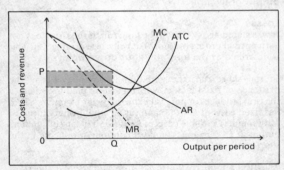

Figure 16. Equilibrium of the firm in an imperfect market

It can be seen from Figure 16 that the firm's output will be OQ, its price OP and that it will earn supernormal profits equal to the shaded area.

Supernormal profits have an allocative function: they attract new firms into an industry. As new firms enter, the demand curves of existing firms shift to the left, and supernormal profits are reduced. In the case of **monopolistic competition** – where there are many sellers with slightly different products in a market, and perfect freedom of entry into the market – only normal profits are earned in the long run, as depicted in Figure 17.

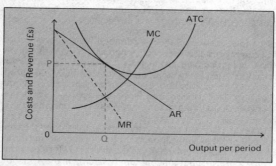

Figure 17. Long run equilibrium in monopolistic competition

Pure monopoly The extreme case of an imperfect market is a pure monopoly, in which there is only one firm in a market and there is no possibility of new entrants. In this case, supernormal profits (as in Figure 16) could persist in the long run.

Of course, the existence of a downward-sloping demand curve does not guarantee that the firm will be able to earn normal profits or more: if ATC is greater than AR at every level of output, the monopolist will cease production in the long run just like any other firm.

Criticisms of traditional theory

Few, if any, markets correspond to the assumptions of traditional theory, but this does not necessarily render it useless. The idea of theorizing is to abstract the essential characteristics of a market and to examine the implications of these. As most firms do face a downward-sloping demand curve and do have an eye to profitability, the traditional theory is a relevant starting point. It provides us, for example, with an idea of the significance of barriers to the entry of new firms, and shows that (in the case of long run equilibrium in monopolistic competition) firms will produce with spare capacity, which indicates a less efficient allocation of resources than might be achieved.

It is sometimes said that firms in actual markets behave as if they were pure monopolies (e.g. where a firm's product is protected by patents) or in monopolistic competition (e.g. some areas of retailing). But perhaps more important, traditional theory acts as a measuring rod: a standard by which the significance of variations from its assumptions can be measured.

The first difficulty with traditional theory is that it is concerned with a single product, single market enterprise. We shall see below how the single market problem can be overcome within the traditional model (see 'price discrimination'), but the multi-product firm does present difficulties since factors may be switched (or shared) between different product lines so that, in determining prices, the allocation of costs to specific products is a problem.

Secondly, traditional theory is limited by its concentration on *current* costs and revenue, whereas it is clear that many firms will price their products with a view to the future; for example, they may hold prices low to build up future demand or to discourage new firms from entering the industry. This criticism may be summarized as a distinction between short run and long run profit maximization.

However, the most telling criticisms centre around the concept of profit maximization itself. Before considering these, it is important to understand that the $MC = MR$ rule is not a behavioural assumption, but simply a mathematical method of representing the fact of profit maximization. Even if entrepreneurs have not heard of marginal revenue or marginal cost, or would not be able to calculate them anyway, it remains a fact that *if* a firm maximizes its profits then its marginal revenue and marginal costs will be equal, *however* they arrived at the profit maximizing price and output.

In his book, '*Theory of the Firm*' (Macmillan, 1973), C.J. Hawkins objects to the single-minded assumption of profit maximization which, he argues, would require the entrepreneur to '. . .work in a damp, dingy office and drive round in a second-hand rubbish truck – if it helped profit by however little. He would cheat, lie and risk the lives of millions of people if only it would make his firm a few extra pennies. . . He would make Al Capone seem like a benevolent uncle'.

What Hawkins seeks to point out is that firms have a range of objectives, which may include not only making profits but also protecting their customers and employees, ensuring quality and reliability of their products, serving the local community, etc. It could, however, be argued that such motives fall within the concept of long run profit maximization.

A second criticism is that a firm cannot know whether it is maximizing profits in any case: how can it tell if another price and output would increase profits without trying it? Such experiments involve the risk of worsening profitability. Thus, it seems more likely that firms will think in terms of a rate of growth of profits or a target level of profitability which they would consider both acceptable and achievable: a different proposition to profit maximization.

A third criticism, with which we commence a brief study of some of the alternatives to traditional theory, is that it is the objectives of managers which determine the pricing and output decisions of firms, and that these may differ from the profit maximizing objectives of the owners.

Managerial utility

In the modern joint stock company, there is commonly a 'divorce' between ownership and control. The management team which controls the day-to-day running of the firm may be quite separate from the shareholders (who collectively own the firm's assets and share in its profits). If the objectives of the managers differ from those of the shareholders, we can predict a different equilibrium output and price when compared with traditional theory.

'Managerial utility' is the term given to the satisfaction derived by management from the achievement of their objectives. These might include, in addition to the job security provided by profits, the number of staff under their control, business perks and discretionary control over peripheral expenditure. Managerial utility is therefore closely linked to the size of the company, and we might therefore expect a tendency to increased output (and therefore lower prices) when compared with the profit maximizing equilibrium.

Sales maximization

If the salaries of managers are more directly related to the firm's turnover than its profits, we would expect the managers to direct the strategy of the firm to the maximization of revenue from sales, rather than profit maximization. This is compatible with the managerial utility theory since it is likely that increased sales will be accompanied by more staff, greater personal prestige and security, increased expenditure on perks and so on. However, there is likely to be a profit constraint: a certain level of profits will be necessary to prevent the disquiet of shareholders (which might threaten the managers' job security). If we assume that this constraint is represented by normal profits, we can compare the predictions of the sales maximization and profit maximization models.

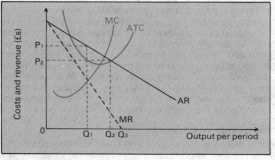

Figure 18. Sales maximization and profit maximization compared

In Figure 18, the profit maximizing output is OQ_1, and the equilibrium price is OP_1. The maximum output a sales maximizing firm would consider is OQ_3 (where $MR = 0$), since beyond this output total revenue would fall. However, in our example, the firm would not earn normal profits at this output. Thus, the sales maximizing firm's equilibrium output will be OQ_2 (where only normal profits are earned), with a corresponding price of OP_2. It can be seen that the sales maximizing firm charges a lower price than a profit maximizer and produces a greater output.

Behavioural theories

Other 'new' theories of the firm concentrate on the importance of the structure of a business organization and its effect on the decision-making process.

Of administrative necessity, a large business organization is split into departments specializing in the various aspects of the firm's activity. This may involve different product groups, each with marketing teams and product development groups, technical managers, finance departments, personnel sections, and so on, possibly spread over a number of different plants in different areas (sometimes in different countries). Each section will have its own goals, just as the firm as a whole does. But the interests of different departments may conflict with each other, or the perception of the firm's overall objectives may differ between these various groups.

The problem then is to resolve these conflicts within the overall goals, and to assess the performance of individual units within the global strategy. This requires the collection of information (which itself adds to the firm's costs) and the formation of an organizational structure which is compatible with the efficient co-ordination of the various elements in the firm. This may be so complex that 'satisficing' rules of thumb need to be established if the firm is to achieve anything at all.

Satisficing incorporates the view that maximization – of anything – is not a practical motive. It is argued that firms will set goals for certain aspects of their activity (e.g. sales volume, revenue, rate of profit). Goals are set which are considered 'realistic', and the management is content if they are successfully achieved. If they are too easily met, the goals may be revised upwards for the future, whilst if they are not achieved, the firm will seek alternative means to the end (and may ultimately revise the goals downwards). To some extent, revision of goals may represent a form of maximizing, but this depends on the degree of ambition embodied in the firm's aspirations in the first place.

Ownership and control

The obvious question raised by these new theories of the firm is why shareholders are prepared to allow the managers' objectives precedence over their own (i.e. profit maximization). There are some compelling reasons:

1. Share prices If it is known that shareholders are dissatisfied with the way the firm is being run, share prices are likely to fall, making the owners vulnerable to capital loss.

2. Information In the absence of our convenient cost and revenue schedules, the shareholders may have no way of knowing that profits could be increased.

3. Information costs The costs of finding such information, replacing the managers, and so on, might be so high as to reduce profits below the level achieved through, for example, sales maximization.

4. Satisficing The shareholders may themselves be satisficers and content themselves with what they consider a satisfactory dividend.

5. Risk avoidance The shareholders may take the rational view that striving for maximum profits would expose the firm to commercial risks which they would prefer to avoid for the sake of their own security.

The new theories of the firm – of which this has of necessity been only a brief and incomplete survey – throw light on some areas which the traditional theory has tended to neglect, such as the separation of ownership and control, the cost of information, conflicting objectives, and the impact of the organizational structure on decision-making. This is not to deny the significance of profits in determining firms' decisions, but to place them within a wider context.

Price discrimination

Definition A situation in which a producer, by separating parts of the total market, charges different consumers a different price for the same product in the same time period, *for reasons other than differences in the cost of production.*

The conditions for price discrimination to be practicable are:

1. The firm must have some degree of monopoly power over the supply of its product.

2. It must be possible to prevent (or make difficult) the resale of goods between markets.

3. The price elasticities of demand in the different markets must be different.

Markets may be separated on the basis of geographical region, consumers' income or social class, domestic as opposed to commercial users, age and so forth.

One of the most obvious uses of price discrimination is to increase the profits of the firm. Figure 19 gives one example of such a situation. The demand curve shown is for its 'principal' market. It can be seen that it can earn normal profits by selling OQ units at a price of OP, and that it is not possible to earn supernormal profits (since the ATC curve does not cut through the AR curve).

It can be seen that the firm has spare capacity, i.e. its equilibrium output is less than its optimum output (where ATC = MC). If the firm produced its optimum output (OQ) and could sell its surplus $(OQ_1 - OQ)$ in a different market at the lower price of OP_1, its total revenue would be the area $OPabcQ_1$, whilst its total costs are OP_1cQ_1, i.e. it is now earning supernormal profits shown by the area P_1Pab.

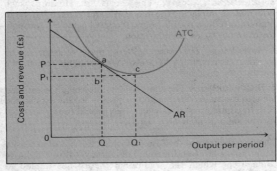

Figure 19. Price discrimination to increase profits

There are many examples of this form of price discrimination. It might, for example, be used to explain why cars produced in the U.K. are sold at lower prices abroad than in the home market (although other factors would have to be taken into account). The principle is simply that of charging the price which the market will bear.

Price discrimination may also be of direct benefit to consumers who would not otherwise be able to afford the product, and may even enable production where normal profits would not otherwise be possible. Thus, although price discrimination may benefit producers by increasing their profits, it may also be directed to the benefit of individual groups of consumers within a market (such as the poor or the elderly), and (as in our example above) it may enable firms to produce at a more efficient level of output, improving the output which society gains from a given set of inputs.

Cost discrimination

One application of the general principle of price discrimination which is widely used is a form of pricing to take account of capacity which would otherwise remain idle. This applies particularly in industries where the firm's capacity is dictated by peak demand but where there are considerable variations in the level of demand (either within the day, between days, or between different periods of the year). Examples range from the telephone, the power supply and transport industries, to holiday camp sites and cinemas.

In such cases, the firm's overheads will be geared to the peak demand, and the good or service will be priced so that normal profits or more are earned. However, this price may stimulate so little demand in the off peak period that it is unprofitable to provide the service outside the peak demand period.

However, since the fixed costs will exist in any case if peak production continues, the logical pricing rule should be derived from the short run shut-down hypothesis. If PED is greater in the off peak period, a lower price will increase the firm's off peak revenue. Provided the off peak revenue more than covers the additional (variable) costs of off peak production, the firm's profits will be increased.

It can be seen that if the firm could not earn normal profits from its peak production, it might still be able to continue production as a result of the contribution of its off peak pricing policy.

Since **off peak pricing** results from differences in the *relevant* costs of production to be considered in determining prices, it has been distinguished here from the formal definition of 'price discrimination' (where pricing is not associated with differences in costs between markets).

Alternative pricing strategies
It is not possible here to consider alternative strategies for determining prices, such as full-cost or rate of return pricing. The book by Davies and Hughes in the 'Further Reading' section is particularly recommended in this context.

Oligopoly
A market in which a few firms dominate the supply is defined as an oligopoly. This definition covers a multitude of possible market situations, and thus it is not surprising that no general theory of oligopoly behaviour has been developed. However, since so many actual markets could be classified as oligopolies, it is important to attempt some generalizations about the type of market behaviour that might be expected.

The main feature of any oligopoly is the interdependence of the firms involved:

1. One firm's decisions will be conditioned by how it *expects* the other firms to react.
2. The outcome of any decision will depend on how the other firms do *in fact* react.
3. Firms within the industry will recognize that their actions may attract new competition from outside firms.

These factors exert a strong pressure towards the maintenance of the *status quo*. The greater the degree of substitutability between the firms' products, and the greater the recognition of their interdependence, the greater are the pressures towards price stability in oligopoly markets. Each firm realizes that an individual attempt to maximize its own share of market profits may result in a price war which decreases the profits of the industry as a whole (and may leave all firms worse off).

It is possible that such pressures towards price stability will be recognized (implicitly or explicitly) in some form of collective pricing strategy:

1. Cartels An agreement between firms on the prices which they will set. One example, where contracts are open to tender, is for the firms in the market to agree to take turns in offering the 'lowest' price for contracts. In this way, each firm is assured of a regular flow of profitable work, without the need to compete against the others by reducing their prices.

2. Price leadership A more subtle form of strategy – where explicit agreement is not necessary – is where firms keep their prices in line with that of the market leader (in the knowledge that the market leader will set a price which enables the 'marginal' firm to earn at least normal profits).

The firms may also tend to operate policies designed to prevent new firms entering an industry:

3. Full-line forcing is when manufacturers will only supply retailers if they will sell the complete range of the firm's products. The costs involved may limit the number of suppliers the retailer can deal with.

4. Exclusive dealing is when the manufacturer prohibits the retailer from selling competitors' products as a condition of supply.

Competition policy
All these forms of agreement would be classified in the U.K. as restrictive trade practices, and as such would need to be registered with the Office of Fair Trading (OFT). Such agreements are considered against the public interest and are generally prohibited unless the parties to the agreement can prove to the Restrictive Practices Court that the agreement does not injure the public interest (e.g. because it guarantees high production standards or more efficient service, or offers employment or trade benefits on a macroeconomic scale). However, such agreements may be difficult to detect or prove, and the number of unregistered agreements which do come to light suggests that the practice is not totally prevented by government legislation.

A firm which accounts for 25% or more of market output (as would be the case for many oligopolists) is also classified in law as a 'monopoly' and subject to the surveillance of the Monopolies and Mergers Commission. This has the power – on reference from the OFT or the Minister – to investigate firms' behaviour in detail. Such an investigation may result in recommendations which require the firm to change its practices and which could be supported by sanctions.

Non-price competition
Despite this, the absence of price competition remains a feature of many oligopoly markets, but it does not mean that

there is a total absence of competition. Non-price competition may take many forms: *actual* differences between products, e.g. quality, styling and reliability, as well as *apparent* differences, e.g. brand images. Some of the implications of this product differentiation have been considered previously (see pages 75–76), but a brief consideration of one of the main elements of non-price competition – advertising – remains necessary.

Advertising

From the firm's viewpoint, an advertising campaign for a particular product might seek to achieve one or more different objectives:

1. **Inform** the consumers of the product's existence or of improvements in it.
2. **Combat** the advertising by producers of substitute products (to 'restore balance').
3. **Persuade** consumers to buy the good in preference to substitutes (or to enter the market for the first time). This serves the dual purpose of both increasing demand and attempting to make it less responsive to price increases (or more responsive to price decreases).
4. **Inhibit** potential new entrants to the industry, both by increasing consumer loyalty and by increasing the promotional expenditure which would be necessary to effect a successful entry.

It is often alleged that advertising acts against the interests of the consumer. For example, it may raise the producers' costs, decrease the consumer's choice (by inhibiting new firms from entering a market), or may simply confuse the real merits of the different firms' goods. In this light it is the consumer who ultimately pays for advertising – in terms of higher prices than would otherwise be necessary.

However, there are significant counter-arguments. If advertising increases the firm's demand, it may be able to gain from economies of larger scale production, which may be passed on to the consumer in the form of lower prices. In this case, it could be argued that advertising promotes a more efficient use of a country's resources (rather than wasting them as is more often argued). This could be supported by the view that advertising as an informative medium improves the consumers' knowledge of the market and enables them to make better use of their incomes. Moreover, a counter to the inhibition argument is that advertising provides the means whereby new firms can enter a market successfully.

Even from this small sample of the many possible arguments, it can be seen that there is no definitive answer, and that individual cases need to be treated on their merits.

Nationalized industries

This chapter has been concerned with output decisions and pricing strategies for firms in the private sector. Quite clearly, different strategies may need to be applied when determining the price and output of goods and services provided directly or indirectly through the state (i.e. public enterprise). There would, for example, be little merit in a state-run profit maximizing national educational service. The market strategies in the public sector must obviously be appropriate to the motives for the public provision of goods.

Nationalized industries are a specific sub-group of the public enterprise sector, i.e. those which are primarily engaged in producing *and selling* goods and services, and consist mainly of corporations in the energy, transport, communications, steel and shipbuilding industries. Motives for their public ownership include the need:

1. To provide for natural monopolies (see page 15).
2. To ensure continuity of production in industries of strategic importance to the economy and consumers.
3. To ensure a standard provision of certain services throughout the economy, which might only be commercial in certain parts of the country.
4. To prevent the abuse of monopoly power by private firms.
5. To permit the structural reorganization of an industry without excessively adverse economic and social effects within particular regions.

The basic premises for the market strategies of nationalized industries are:

1. Pricing Since the resources used by nationalized industries have an opportunity cost, efficient resource allocation requires that prices should be set to achieve a given rate of return on capital employed: this rate of return being the equivalent of our idea of normal profits. The aim is that the nationalized industries should cover their long run costs of production (i.e. including the cost of maintaining and expanding their fixed capital).

Exceptions to this general rule are made where an industry is required to operate non-commercial services in the public interest, or where (as in the airline industry) prices are essentially dictated by world conditions outside the individual industry's control. Also, many of the nationalized industries face market conditions which make off peak pricing viable.

2. Externalities In determining investment and pricing strategies, nationalized industries may be required to take specific account of the social costs and benefits resulting from their decisions.

In practice, the market strategies of nationalized industries are an economic mine field, full of explosive arguments which more often than not belong in the political rather than the economic arena.

Chapter 9

Factor Markets

Throughout this book references have been made to factor markets, factor prices and factor mobility. We have, for example, considered the role of profits – the return to the factor, enterprise – in some detail, as well as the effects of wage costs on price competitiveness. Interest, the return to capital, has also featured quite prominently (in relation to the balance of payments and exchange rates, for example). Thus, in this concluding chapter, we bring some of these strands of analysis together in a brief consideration of the markets for scarce productive resources and, in particular, the labour market.

Resource allocation

Factor markets bring together the buyers and sellers of productive resources: land, labour, capital and enterprise. Just as in the product markets, the interaction of these buyers and sellers results in the formation of prices, which serve an allocative role within the economy. As the price paid for a factor service rises, we would expect factors to be attracted away from alternative uses. The price acts not only as a signal to the owners of the factor services, but also as a means of rationing the available supply between the potential buyers.

Derived demand

Factors are not wanted for their own sake, but for the contribution they can make to the productive process, i.e. they are in derived demand. Ultimately, the demand for a factor depends on the demand for the product which it is used to make.

Market prices

A competitive factor market can be depicted in much the same way as a competitive product market: the intersection of the demand and supply curves forming the market price. Adjustments of the equilibrium result from changes in the conditions of demand and supply. For example, an increase in demand for the end-product will increase the demand for the factors used in producing the good, causing market price to rise, *ceteris paribus*.

Factor substitution

Since, in the long run, there are usually different ways of producing the good (by combining factors in different proportions), a rise in the price of one factor may eventually increase the demand for substitutes. For example, an increase in wage rates may encourage a firm to replace labour with capital in its productive process.

Marginal revenue product (MRP) is defined as the addition to a firm's revenue resulting from selling the extra output produced by increasing the employment of a factor by one unit, *ceteris paribus*. MRP depends on the marginal

product of the additional factor (subject to the law of diminishing returns) and the effect of increasing output on the market price of the good.

The equilibrium level of employment of a factor would thus be where the addition to the firm's costs when employing an extra unit of a factor (i.e. marginal cost) is equal to that factor's MRP. Employing more units of the factor would detract from the firm's profits (since the additional factor adds more to costs than revenue), and employing less units would indicate forgone profits. Having determined the equilibrium level of employment of a factor, the supply curve will indicate the price which would make that quantity available.

THE LABOUR MARKET

However, if it is accepted that this form of traditional analysis is somewhat questionable in explaining some types of product market, it is quite certain that the theory is an inadequate basis for understanding labour markets. At an elementary level, it can be criticized on the following grounds:

1. MRP theory is based on the assumption of a profit maximizing motive. We have seen that there are good grounds for questioning such an assumption.

2. There are many labour markets where it would be quite impossible to measure the marginal product of labour, e.g. public services.

3. Labour is often combined in fixed quantity with other factors, and thus it is difficult to distinguish the specific contribution of labour.

4. Labour does not consist of identical units: even where skill levels are roughly the same, there may be significant differences in attitude and application between different workers.

5. Wages are not the only determinant of labour supply. Workers will be influenced by such aspects of a job as loyalty to an employer, family tradition, working conditions, social acceptability, perks and so forth.

Beyond these criticisms (which can be overcome to some extent by adapting the way in which MRP theory is applied), there are certain features of labour markets which distinguish them from other markets to such an extent that traditional analysis may be thought totally inappropriate.

1. Strikes Organized labour has won the right to withdraw labour in pursuance of an industrial dispute, whilst being able effectively to prevent the employer from hiring alternative sources of labour supply. From the economic viewpoint, such action may have far-reaching effects of a staggering magnitude. During the 1970s, strike action brought about a period in which manufacturing industry was only able to function for three days a week, and accounted (according to most commentators) for the downfall of at least two governments.

2. Equity One of the important elements in any wage settlement is the concept of 'fairness': a notion which is virtually impossible to gauge objectively.

3. Comparative wages One method of attempting to establish fairness is to make comparisons between different groups of workers. Thus, an important element in many wage negotiations is comparison by means of relativities and differentials. **Differentials** measure the differences in wage rates between different groups of workers within a company, and are usually related to skill levels. **Relativities** are comparisons, between either firms or industries, with workers with similar skill levels, working conditions, training periods, etc.

4. Complementary costs From the employer's viewpoint, the cost of labour does not simply comprise the wage paid. It also encompasses the provision of amenities to meet various government regulations, the employment of personnel specialists, payments to government (such as National Insurance contributions by the employer), and so on. Moreover, government legislation can impose costs associated with dismissing labour, such as required redundancy payments.

Given this analysis, it might be thought that the dice are exclusively loaded in favour of the suppliers of labour. Certainly, the bargaining power of labour has increased quite remarkably with the growth of trade unions, assisted by a more favourable political environment, but it should not be forgotten that employers are equally capable of combining together and that their resources to support a bargaining position are equally strong in many cases. Particularly during periods of relatively high unemployment, employers may present a wage ultimatum supported by the threat of redundancies. Thus, it is argued that wage determination is essentially a matter of bargaining, and therefore the outcome depends to a large extent on the relative strengths of the parties to an agreement.

Collective bargaining

Roughly three-quarters of all workers' wages are negotiated under conditions of collective bargaining, typically between trade unions and employers in a particular industry. These normally establish basic minimum wage-rates and conditions of employment, which may then be subject to further negotiation at local level (to take into account the conditions affecting particular plants and firms). Wage negotiations are often extremely complex, highly dependent on agreements and principles established in past negotiations, and totally specific to the conditions prevailing in a particular industry. The process is complicated by the range of factors which are often negotiated within the bargaining arena: not only wage-rates but holiday entitlements, pension rights, working hours, productivity, working conditions and so forth.

The following is a very brief summary of the factors which most commonly come into the reckoning in wage negotiations:

1. Changes in the cost of living (i.e. inflation).
2. Profitability of the firm or industry.
3. Existence of labour shortages in a market (or of excess labour supply, i.e. unemployment).
4. Productivity.
5. Differentials and relativities.
6. Nature of the job, e.g. physical working conditions.
7. Government policy, e.g. incomes policies.
8. Peripheral bargaining factors, e.g. new management or union negotiators or political events.

Industrial disputes

The vast majority of wage bargaining reaches a conclusion which is acceptable to all parties. In most cases, machinery is available – such as an arbitration panel – to settle elements of a negotiation which cannot be decided through the usual negotiations. The government sponsors the Advisory, Conciliation and Arbitration Service (ACAS) which can be used to assist in settling a variety of industrial relations problems.

Strikes However, a certain number of negotiations end in deadlock with no mutually acceptable basis for arbitration, in which case unions may seek the support of their members in strike action. According to the Department of Employment, 98% of all manufacturing plants in the U.K. are completely free of strikes in any one year. Between 1961 and 1978, strike action caused an average annual loss of less than half a day per employee in the U.K.

Quantitatively, therefore, the significance of strikes should not be allowed to get out of proportion. Far more working days are lost through industrial injury, sickness, and absenteeism than through strikes. However, the official figures do not account for the knock-on effects of strikes on other plants and industries, for strikes lasting less than a day (which may be repeated day after day) or for other alternatives to the outright strike, such as overtime bans, working-to-rule, or the go-slow.

Costs The cost of strikes is measured in official statistics in terms of working days lost (and hence implied forgone output). However, the costs should really be considered in much broader terms, and as they affect different interests:

1. **The business sector** To the firm directly involved, the

obvious cost is in terms of forgone profits and overhead costs, but if production is interrupted over a lengthy period or at frequent intervals, orders may be lost and customers may change to alternative suppliers in the future. Also, because of the extent of the division of labour, the effects on other firms (not directly involved in the dispute) may be severe. A small group of workers, such as those in the electricity supply industry, for example, have the potential to stop production in a vast number of other industries.

2. The government The families of workers who are on strike are entitled to claim welfare benefits in case of financial hardship, which increases government expenditure. This may imply higher taxes or increased borrowing (or decreased expenditure in other areas), with the consequences we have previously analysed. The political costs may be more far-reaching.

3. The union The union (under current legislation) is assumed to pay £12 per week to each of its members on strike: a prolonged dispute could represent a severe financial burden. More directly, the workers and their families will suffer severely reduced incomes for the duration of the strike, and may face difficulties in meeting their financial commitments.

4. The public Apart from interrupted supplies of certain goods and services, people outside the industry directly involved may suffer from secondary lay-offs.

5. The economy Clearly, strikes result in the economy's output being less than would be possible, and this inevitably means lower living standards than could have been achieved.

The parties to a dispute are, of course, faced with the direct costs of the strike, but may not take account of the social costs of their actions. Generally speaking, strikes are a primitive and often inefficient means of conducting a dispute; 'victories' are often won only at the cost of subsequent unemployment and lost profits, and not only in the firms directly involved. However, moves to restructure the negotiating procedure have met with little success, leaving many commentators with a view that a more fundamental challenge, such as a restructuring of the ownership and decision-making processes in industry, must be faced.

Further Reading

General texts

Harbury, C., *Economic Behaviour: An Introduction* (George Allen & Unwin, 1980)

Maile, R., *Key Facts Passbook: G.C.E. A-Level Economics* (Letts, revised edition, 1983)

Nevin, E., *Textbook of Economic Analysis* (Macmillan, fifth edition, 1978)

Stanlake, G., *Macro-economics: an introduction* (Longman, second edition, 1979)

Applied texts

N.I.E.S.R., *The United Kingdom Economy* (Heinemann Educational Books, second edition, 1979)

Prest, A. and Coppock, D. (eds.), *The U.K. Economy: A Manual of Applied Economics* (Weidenfeld & Nicolson, 1980)

Tree, N., *The Year in Review* (Anforme Ltd., annually)

Specific texts

Beckerman, W., *An Introduction to National Income Analysis* (Weidenfeld & Nicolson, second edition, 1976)

Cobham, D., *The Economics of International Trade* (Woodhead-Faulkner, 1979)

Davies, B., *The United Kingdom and the World Monetary System* (Heinemann Educational Books, third revised edition, 1979)

Davies, J. and Hughes, S., *Pricing in Practice* (Heinemann Educational Books, 1975)

Hawkins, C., *Theory of the Firm* (Macmillan, 1978)

Hawkins, K., *Unemployment* (Penguin, 1979)

Rees, A., *The Economics of Work and Pay* (Harper & Row, second edition, 1979)

Trevithick, J., *Inflation: A Guide to the Crisis in Economics* (Penguin, 1979)

Turvey, R., *Demand and Supply* (George Allen & Unwin, second edition, 1980)

Utton, M., *Industrial Concentration* (Penguin, 1970)

Statistics

Official statistics are presented in various monthly and annual publications, published by H.M.S.O., including:
Annual Abstract of Statistics
Economic Trends (monthly)
Monthly Digest of Statistics
National Income and Expenditure
Regional Statistics
United Kingdom Balance of Payments

Worked examples

Maile, R., *Worked Examples for A-Level Economics* (Letts, 1983)

Watts, M. and Glew, M., *Topics and Objectives in A-Level Economics* (Heinemann Educational Books, 1975)

Glossary

Absolute advantage Trade theory model, in which one producer is more efficient in the production of one good, and the other producer is more efficient in the production of another, so that complete specialization and subsequent trade can prove mutually beneficial.

Accelerator principle The principle demonstrates the exaggerated effect on net investment (and hence production in the capital goods sector) of changes in the rate of change of consumer demand (or national income).

Aggregate monetary demand The total planned expenditure of consumers, firms, government and foreigners, on goods and services which are produced within an economy (net of any indirect taxes or import components).

Automatic stabilizers Aspects of government expenditure and taxation which counteract the trend in economic activity without the need for policy changes, by altering the level of *aggregate monetary demand*, e.g. unemployment benefits, which prevent incomes falling as fast as they otherwise would in a recession.

Balanced budget A change in fiscal policy in which the change in taxation is exactly offset by an opposite change in the level of government expenditure.

Balance of payments An annual statement of the currency flow resulting from transactions between the residents of one country and residents in other countries. 'Residents' include consumers, firms and government.

Balance of trade Sub-division of the *balance of payments* showing the net inflow ('surplus') or outflow ('deficit') of currency as a result of international transactions of goods (only).

Black economy see *hidden economy*

Black market Illegal exchange of goods and services above a controlled or administered maximum price (resulting from excess demand).

Brand proliferation Where firms produce what is essentially the same good under a variety of trade names, often distinguishing the goods' images through advertising.

Buffer stock A store of excess supply, where a minimum price is reached in a controlled market, which may be used to prevent prices rising above a certain level in the event of future excess demand.

Business cycles Observed fluctuations in the level of economic activity over time.

Capacity output see *optimum output*

Capital The stock of goods which are not used for current consumption and which contribute to future consumption. This comprises producer single-use and durable-use goods, work in progress and stocks of unsold consumer goods.

Cartel An agreement between producers to fix the price in a market.

Ceteris paribus Literally 'other things being equal'.

Circular flow of income Model depicting the flow of payments for the use of factor services and the flow of payments for produced goods and services between households and the business sector.

Collective goods Goods and services which cannot be restricted in supply to those people prepared to pay for them, e.g. national defence.

Comparative advantage Trade theory showing that mutually beneficial trade is possible even when one producer is more efficient than another in the production of all goods and services.

Competitive demand Where one good is considered a substitute for another.

Conditions of demand The factors which influence the quantity demanded of a good at any given price, such as the prices of other goods, consumer incomes and tastes and preferences.

Conditions of supply The factors which affect the quantity supplied of a good at any given price, such as the cost of productive factors or the number of firms in an industry.

Consumer durable A good which gives services to a consumer over a period of time, e.g. washing machines.

Consumption The process of using up a good or service.

Cost discrimination Where a producer charges different prices to different consumers of the same good for reasons which are associated with differences in the cost of supply.

Cost-push inflation An inflationary process which is initiated by an autonomous increase in the costs of production.

Cyclical unemployment Where resources are unused as a result of aggregate demand being less than aggregate supply.

Deflationary gap The amount by which aggregate monetary demand is inadequate to achieve equilibrium at the full employment level of national income.

Demand The quantity of a good or service which consumers are able and willing to buy in a given market, during a given time period, *ceteris paribus*.

Demand management Government policies designed to control the level of *aggregate monetary demand* in an economy.

Depreciation Of investment, a gradual using up of the value of a capital good ('capital consumption'); of currency, a fall in the value of a currency under a floating exchange rate regime.

Derived demand Where the demand for a factor service (or a good) depends on the demand for the end-product which it is used to produce.

Differentials (of wages) Differences in wage rates paid to different employees doing different jobs for the same employer, usually related to varying skill levels.

Diminishing returns (Law of) As successive units of an identical variable factor are combined with a fixed quantity of other factors, there will come a point where the extra output starts to fall and continues to do so as more units of the variable factor are applied.

Direct tax Amount levied by government on the incomes of individuals and firms, and on transfers of income and wealth.

Diseconomies of scale Where unit production costs rise as the firm's capacity is increased.

Division of labour The separation of the production process of a good into different stages and carried out by different workers: specialization.

Economic growth The rate of change of real *national income* per head. Used theoretically: increases in the economy's full employment level of output.

Elasticity of demand The responsiveness of the quantity demanded to a change in another variable: most commonly, the price elasticity of demand, which is defined as the responsiveness of the quantity demanded to a change in price in a given market during a given period of time, *ceteris paribus*. Other measures may be related to income or the prices of other goods ('cross elasticity of demand').

Elasticity of supply The responsiveness of the quantity supplied to a change (usually) in price, in a given market during a given period of time, *ceteris paribus*.

Enterprise The factor which bears the risk of production: most notably the risk that costs of production will exceed the firm's revenue, so that the entrepreneur receives a negative return, i.e. a 'loss'.

Equilibrium A situation of balance achieved when objectives are realized, so that there is no incentive to change the prevailing situation (other things being equal). Hence:

Equilibrium output The output at which the firm achieves its objectives: usually assumed to be profit maximization or loss minimization (in which case, the equilibrium output is where marginal cost is equal to marginal revenue).

Equilibrium price The market-clearing price at which the demand for a product is exactly matched by the supply.

Exchange rate The price of one country's currency denominated in terms of another country's currency.

Exclusive dealing A restrictive trade practice in which a manufacturer supplies a retailer on condition that the retailer does not sell the products of given competitors.

Externalities Costs and benefits arising from the consumption or production of a good or service affecting people other than those directly involved in the production or purchase of the good. Often referred to as social costs and benefits.

Factor mobility The ease with which factors can be transferred, e.g. occupational mobility–moving from one type of job to another–or geographical mobility–moving from one location to another.

Fiscal policy Deliberate actions of government to change the planned levels of taxation and government expenditure. A central feature of Keynesian *demand management* techniques.

Fixed costs The cost of those factors which cannot be altered in the short run, such as depreciation and interest payments on long-term borrowing. Such costs are often referred to as 'overheads'. The larger the firm's output, the smaller its average fixed costs: spreading overheads.

Floating exchange rate An *exchange rate* whose price is permitted to vary over time, as conditions of demand and supply change.

Free goods Goods which have no *opportunity cost,* e.g. air.

Frictional unemployment A voluntary form of unemployment as people move from one job to another.

Full-line forcing A restrictive trade practice in which a producer requires a retailer or wholesaler to stock the full range of the manufacturer's products, as a condition of supply.

Geographical mobility see *factor mobility.*

Giffen good A special case of an *inferior good* in which the negative *income effect* outweighs the *substitution effect* resulting in a 'perverse' *price effect,* i.e. the quantity demanded expands as price rises, or contracts as price falls.

Gross Domestic Product (GDP) The total output of goods and services accounted for by domestic factor services in a country during a year (which is equal to the total of incomes arising from production within the economy).

Gross National Product (GNP) The total of incomes arising from production within the economy, and the ownership by residents of foreign assets. GNP is equal to GDP plus *net property income from abroad.*

Hidden economy Economic activity which is concealed from the authorities, either because the activity is illegal or in order to avoid tax payments or to enable illegitimate claims for welfare payments. (Sometimes referred to as the 'black economy'.)

Import penetration The proportion of the sales of a good within a country which are accounted for by goods produced in other countries.

Income effect With a fixed money income, a change in the price of a good will alter both the real income of the consumer (income effect) and the relative prices of the goods (substitution effect). For example, when the price of a good falls, *ceteris paribus,* the consumer's real income rises, since he could buy the same amount of goods as before and still have money left over.

Income elasticity of demand The responsiveness of the quantity demanded to a change in incomes, in a given market during a given period of time, *ceteris paribus.* A positive income elasticity (more bought when incomes rise) denotes a *normal good,* and a negative income elasticity (less bought when incomes rise) denotes an *inferior good.*

Incomes policy An attempt to control the rate of change of money wages (or earnings) by constraining the collective bargaining process. The purpose is to control inflation without having to increase unemployment. The policy may be statutory or voluntary, and may relate to other incomes than wages.

Indirect taxes A tax on expenditure, the value-added in the production process or on imports. Licence fees are often included as a sub-group of indirect taxes.

Inferior good A good with a negative *income effect.*

Inflation The process of a generalized and persistent increase in the price-level. The inflation rate is usually measured as the annual rate of increase of the *Retail Price Index.*

Inflationary gap The amount by which *aggregate monetary demand* is greater than that necessary to achieve a full employment equilibrium level of national income.

Injections Autonomous inflows into the *circular flow of income,* comprising (in the full model of income determination) investment, government expenditure and export sales.

Invisibles International trade term for transactions of services, payments of interest, profits and dividends, and for 'transfers' (such as the government's contributions to international organizations).

Joint demand Where goods are used in conjunction to satisfy a want, they are described as 'complements' or goods in joint demand. Hence, an increase in the demand for one good would be expected to be accompanied by an increase in the demand for its complement.

Keynesian policy Followers (sometimes quite remote) of the policies advocated by John Maynard Keynes (1883–1946) whose most influential work was the *'General Theory of Employment, Interest and Money'* (1936). In simple terms, Keynesians argue for the use of *fiscal policy* as the most direct means of controlling the level of *aggregate monetary demand* to influence the level of output and employment.

Labour A factor of production which may be defined as the mental and physical effort of humans in the course of production.

Land A factor of production which encompasses 'Nature's Bounty', i.e. not just the ground, but those things which grow naturally on it or are found naturally underneath it, as well as the gases of the atmosphere and the properties of the sea and sea-bed.

Leakages Flows of money out of a country's *circular flow of income,* comprising tax payments, savings and expenditure on imports.

Long run A conceptual term, not representing a specific chronological period, defined as the period in which the firm can vary the quantities of all its factors (subject to constant technology).

Macroeconomics The division of economic study which is concerned with aggregates: the economy as a whole rather than individual elements of it. For example, macroeconomics would be concerned with total consumption expenditure rather than with an individual consumer's demand.

Managerial utility The basis of a 'new' theory of the firm, which concentrates on the possible differences between the objectives of managers of a firm and those of its shareholders. It considers that managers may be influenced by motives such as personal prestige, power and perks, which may conflict with the (normally assumed) objective of profit maximization.

Marginal analysis Much of *microeconomics* is based on the idea of decisions made at the margin. The margin is the rate at which the total changes; hence, marginal cost is the rate of change of total cost as output changes, for example.

Marginal revenue product (MRP) The additional revenue received by an employer from selling the extra output which results from employing an additional unit of a variable factor.